SOCIAL NETWORKING

The Essence of Innovation

Jay Liebowitz

The Scarecrow Press, Inc.
Lanham, Maryland • Toronto • Plymouth, UK
2007

SCARECROW PRESS, INC.

Published in the United States of America
by Scarecrow Press, Inc.
A wholly owned subsidiary of
The Rowman & Littlefield Publishing Group, Inc.
4501 Forbes Boulevard, Suite 200, Lanham, Maryland 20706
www.scarecrowpress.com

Estover Road
Plymouth PL6 7PY
United Kingdom

British Library Cataloguing in Publication Information Available

Library of Congress Cataloging-in-Publication Data

Liebowitz, Jay, 1957–
   Social networking : the essence of innovation / Jay Liebowitz.
     p. cm.
   Includes bibliographical references and index.
   ISBN-13: 978-0-8108-5857-2 (pbk. : alk. paper)
   ISBN-10: 0-8108-5857-6 (pbk. : alk. paper)
  1. Organizational sociology. 2. Social networks. 3. Business networks. 4.
Knowledge management. I. Title.
HM786.L54 2007
302.3'5—dc22

                2006036876

∞™ The paper used in this publication meets the minimum requirements of
American National Standard for Information Sciences—Permanence of
Paper for Printed Library Materials, ANSI/NISO Z39.48-1992.
Manufactured in the United States of America.

To Janet, Jason, Kenny, Mazel, and my parents—my love for you is unsurpassed.

To all my colleagues and friends whom I have met through social networking.

To Johns Hopkins University and Scarecrow Press—the people in these organizations would be hard to match.

CONTENTS

1 Social Networking: Developing Personal
Knowledge Networks   1

2 Linking Social Networking to Innovation   11

3 Strategic Intelligence: The Synergy of Knowledge
Management, Business Intelligence, and
Competitive Intelligence   21

4 Social Network Analysis: An Introduction   31

5 Using Social Network Analysis in ORG: A Case Study   41

6 Knowledge Mapping Using Social Network Analysis   51

7 Applying Social Networking in Organizations   61

8 Social Network Analysis for Cross-Generational
Knowledge Flows   67

9 A Glimpse beyond Social Networking   73

Appendix   Securities and Exchange Commission: Some
Progress Made on Strategic Human
Capital Management   79

v

References	117
Index	121
About the Author	129

❶

SOCIAL NETWORKING: DEVELOPING PERSONAL KNOWLEDGE NETWORKS

THE PREAMBLE

How many times have you been invited to a party or professional gathering and then told to network? Meeting friends, making acquaintances, and being introduced to friends of friends are all forms of social networking. Some people may not be experts in a particular field; however, the strength of their relationship knowledge—that is, knowing who to go to to get the answers to questions—may give them a competitive edge. In "who knows whom" versus "who knows what," the value of the former should not be overlooked.

Research shows that it's the informal networks, not the formal organizational chart or wire diagrams, that produce the valued-added benefits. In an organization, informal networks could be comprised of people who chat at the coffeepot or watercooler, people who regularly walk together at lunchtime, or people who visit and know one another across departments. Making connections through these informal settings can increase an individual's "organizational intelligence."

Who is one of the most powerful people in an organization? People will answer the president, the chief executive officer (CEO), the chairman of the board, or their boss. One person is often overlooked, however: the assistant or secretary to the president or CEO. This person arranges meetings with the president or CEO, and serves as the gate-keeper to that executive. He or she can help other individuals in an organization greatly if he or she wants. Developing a social network with the administrative staff in the organization can be a wonderful and enriching learning experience. Doing so will also give an individual an inside look at the organization.

One key mantra that should be practiced throughout an organization is that *everyone* is to be treated with respect. Unfortunately, as some people move up the ladder in an organization, they become less tolerant of those who are further down the rungs. This is distressing, as everyone should extend to others the same respect that he or she expects to receive from others. Whether he or she is addressing the housekeeping staff, a secretary, a mail clerk, payroll assistants, managers, directors, or executives, a true professional treats everyone with dignity.

Take, as an example of the good that can come with treating everyone fairly and with respect, the true story of a young student who interned as a mail clerk in a six hundred–person organization. Even though he was the low man on the totem pole, his boss two levels up always treated him with the utmost respect. The student joined the organization as a full-time employee and eventually earned various advanced degrees. He was slowly promoted, and after fifteen years became president of the organization. He remembered from the days of being a mail clerk that this boss had always treated him with dignity and professional courtesy. When he was looking for a senior vice president, he didn't hesitate in asking this former boss to serve in the senior vice president position and be a strong contributing member to the organization.

This story, told by one of my professors in personnel/human resources management classes nearly thirty years ago, left a permanent mark in my mind. It is a poignant lesson in the value of courtesy and respect. It also sheds light on social networking: being civil, respectful, and affable allows an individual to more easily be part of a social network.

Of course, there are social networks that are more closed than others. Whether it is the executive dining room, the country club, or the faculty club, social networks amass in several varieties. There could be social networks of people with a similar trait of being nasty, for example, or a social network that gains pleasure in hostile takeovers of companies. This group of people may have certain characteristics that differ from the characteristics of those in other types of social network groups. Even the mindset of "being on a team" or "being part of the club" connotes certain types of social network characteristics. In this type of social network, if you are not "part of the team," you will be perceived as an outsider and this could affect your relationships with others. Thus, social networks can be perceived as being positively charged, negatively charged, or a combination of the two.

Both power and knowledge can be derived from social networking. Take, for instance, the adage "strength in numbers." Being part of a social network, perhaps in the form of an online community with hundreds of members, could allow an individual to gain influence through others. Perhaps someone wants to "push" an idea in a certain direction; an online community could provide a forum in which to discuss the merits of the proposal and quickly disseminate the idea to many others throughout the online community. At the same time, the individual would gain knowledge through these interactions and collaborative sessions, as people might provide suggestions on refining different ideas.

WHAT IS A SOCIAL NETWORK?

A social network is a set of relationships between a group of "actors" (the "actors" could be individuals, departments, and so on) who usually have similar interests. For example, a website called *Facebook* (www.facebook.com) was developed by Harvard University students to allow students from different colleges or within a given college to form social networks. This is especially useful to students who want to meet people with similar interests the summer before starting college. A student can form a social network in *Facebook* to meet others who have similar interests in athletics, academics, music, theater, or social/extracurricular activities. Someone else can form a social network with those in the college who have had reconstructive knee surgery in order to learn from and meet them. In order to ensure that these social networks aren't compromised, people are typically invited to join.

Through social networks, an individual's outreach is enlarged and the potential for learning is enhanced. For example, *Blackboard* (at www.blackboard.com) is courseware that allows an individual to collaborate, post documents, create group pages, send e-mail to individuals or groups, and the like. *Blackboard* facilitates e-learning and allows students to learn from each other, as well as enables interactions with the faculty or guests within the *Blackboard* framework. The student's personal knowledge is increased by learning from others and integrating others' views and work with personal thoughts. With synergy, the whole is greater than the sum of its parts. In general, an individual's knowledge is heightened through the access to the collective knowledge of others provided through these social networks.

Social network analysis (SNA) is a technique used to map relationships between "actors" in order to determine the strengths of their relationships. For example, if one multinational corporation acquires another multinational firm, SNA could be used to look at the social networks created between the employees some time after the acquisition. IBM performed such an analysis, examining executive interactions, after a multinational corporate merging took place. Social network analysis developed from the social sciences—sociology, anthropology, education, and so on—and can help organizations better understand knowledge flows, knowledge gaps, collaboration networks, social networks, and employee interactions. Social network analysis will be discussed in an upcoming chapter in this book.

PERSONAL KNOWLEDGE NETWORKS

Personal knowledge networks can be defined as connections between individuals that allow the individuals to gain and disperse intelligence. Personal knowledge networks result from interactions and collaboration with others, and they are divided into three primary forms:

1. A line network, which takes the form A-B-C-D, with A, B, C, and D representing different individuals. In this network, individual B would have a direct link to A and C and an indirect link to D.
2. A circle or ring network, which is circular and forms a closed loop.
3. A star network, wherein branches that connect people emanate from the various individuals in the network.

A personal knowledge line network can be compared to the childhood game of "telephone." This game involves telling someone, by word of mouth, a few sentences as a story. That person then tells the next person the same story, and that person then passes it on to the next. This continues down the line of participants until the last person in the line is told the story. Invariably, due to noise caused by interpersonal biases and communications challenges, the end story is somewhat different from the original. Usually, the further a person in the line is from the originator of the story (or the greater the number of people between the originator and a given person), the more distorted the story is. This equates to a line network wherein those who are directly connected exchange more accurate knowledge than those who are more loosely connected within the network.

The circle or ring network is a closed loop, meaning that "what goes around, comes around." To continue with the telephone example used above, in a circle network, the last person who was given the story would then pass the description back to the originator of the story and the loop could continue. In an organizational setting, the personal knowledge network structured around a ring can provide fluid communications flow between people in the network, although it can also require some extra time for spreading the word, depending on the size of the network.

The star structure network might be viewed as a snowball effect to networking. In a star network, one individual tells those within his or her network of friends something. Thereafter each of those friends tells others in his or her network of friends, and so on. The path continues, with a resultant star-shape effect. The communication patterns that emanate from individuals take a shape similar to that of a spur on a cowboy's boot and can be thought of as "spurring" knowledge sharing.

As there are different types of networks, there are also different categories of knowledge. One common categorization is tacit versus explicit. "Tacit" refers to the knowledge that people have in their heads; once it is codified, it becomes "explicit." Eliciting someone's tacit knowledge is challenging, though some knowledge acquisition approaches can be used. Effective approaches may include structured and unstructured interviews, protocol analysis (verbal walk-throughs where the expert talks aloud when solving a problem), observation, and others. Tacit knowledge can be procedural (such as IF-THEN rules) or declarative (descriptive, such as concept maps, cases, scripts, objects, etc.). Lessons learned or best practices can be represented either as procedural or declarative knowledge. Rules of thumb (heuristics acquired through experiential learning) or quick tips can easily be represented as IF-THEN rules.

Knowledge can also be described as sticky and fluid. People define "sticky" and "fluid" in different ways. Sticky is what gets "stuck" with an individual, while "fluid" knowledge flows easily from one person to another. A combination between the two may be called "syrupy," and would describe knowledge that is sticky but still able to flow between people.

Why should personal knowledge networks be encouraged in organizations? The simple reason is that companies must be agile and adaptive to compete in today's competitive marketplace, and the key way of surviving is through knowledge. Personal knowledge networks contribute to organizational learning by allowing individuals to become more productive and facile by knowing who and what they need to maximize their effectiveness and how to do it. Their personal knowledge networks can be applied to help build the institutional memory of the organization and allow the organization to be proactive versus reactive. Consider how many lessons-learned systems fail due to passive analysis and dissemination of the lessons (versus active analysis and dissemination). Instead of using a "pull" approach, a "push" approach—pushing the right lessons to the right people at the right time—allows the lessons-learned process to be timely and effective. In the same manner, if personal knowledge networks are proactive, more timely knowledge sharing and dissemination can improve the organization's overall effectiveness and efficiency.

HOW DO PERSONAL KNOWLEDGE NETWORKS GET BUILT?

Personal knowledge networks in organizations are built in various ways. One approach is through friends or individuals in other departments within an organization. These friends or individuals act as liaisons between departments and groups. These individuals are "boundary spanners"; they allow an individual to network with other groups in the organization. Another personal knowledge network may consist of program coordinators in all or several of the various departments in an organization. Access to this network could provide an individual with quick access to information and knowledge that otherwise would be compartmentalized. Integrating across these functional silos is a key part of knowledge management, whereby these personal knowledge networks can be built and used effectively.

Another approach for building a personal knowledge network is through cliques—friends of friends. In the above example, an individual may not be a direct part of the program coordinator network, but may have a friend who is. Thus, through a friend or "friend of a friend" ("cliques" in SNA parlance), an individual can establish and increase his or her personal knowledge network.

Online communities, discussion groups, blogs, and chat rooms are other mechanisms for building personal knowledge networks. These modes allow birds of a feather, so to speak, to get together in cyberspace to learn from each other. In an organizational context, electronic meeting spaces allow people with similar interests to easily share ideas and knowledge without the obstruction of organizational walls.

Professional societies and related activities can also be wonderful ways to develop a personal knowledge network. Conferences and workshops sponsored by professional societies can increase an individual's knowledge, as well as broaden the individual's network of professional colleagues. For example, the Society of Competitive Intelligence Professionals has over eighty-six hundred members worldwide. The members are mainly practitioners, educators, and interested parties in the field of competitive intelligence. The society maintains a website (www.scip.org) that offers discussion boards, job postings, CI publications, CI conferences, seminars, and education courses, and other opportunities to further link and build the members' personal knowledge networks. The society also offers more traditional conferences, chapter meetings, and so on.

Cross-functional teaming, cross-staffing, cross-departmental meetings, mentoring programs, and informal get-togethers (such as knowledge fairs, mixers, and so on) provide settings in which knowledge can be shared and knowledge networks can be built within an organization.

These endeavors can integrate across the functional silos of the organization and create more widespread social networks, which has the further effect of allowing knowledge to be disseminated more broadly within the organization.

WHY ARE PERSONAL KNOWLEDGE NETWORKS SO IMPORTANT?

Have you ever felt not "connected"? That is, have you ever felt a bit isolated, either professionally or personally? Not every person is people oriented, but most people crave having someone with whom they can share thoughts, exchange ideas, and build camaraderie. Whether by going out to lunch with some colleagues or working as part of a project team, most knowledge workers seem to enjoy reaching out to others. In some instances, personal knowledge networks may serve as exchanges, where new ideas for fostering innovation are bounced around, and at other times, these networks may be the place for catharsis, where people can clear their thoughts.

When I joined NASA Goddard Space Flight Center as their knowledge management officer, spawning and nurturing personal knowledge networks became an important part of my job. It was important that I connect people to others to stimulate ideas, to create collaborating teams, or simply to make an individual's day seem more meaningful and enjoyable. Personally, I joined a creative learning group that allowed me to connect with others outside of my specific directorate and helped me to get a better sense for what was happening across the NASA Center. It also fostered some wonderful lasting relationships that improved my own work and helped me establish professional friendships across the Center. If I hadn't reached out beyond my own department, I would have been swallowed up in a microcosm and would not have been able to be as effective as a knowledge management officer in sharing and disseminating knowledge.

In Charlene Li's Forrester Research report titled "Profiles: The Real Value of Social Networks" (July 15, 2004, at www.forrester.com/Research/Document/Excerpt/0,7211,34432,00.html), Li indicates that as social networks mature, they will grow into three main groups: "1) communication networks dominated by portals; 2) affinity networks based on relationships; and 3) interest-based networks focused on a shared passion." The portal technologies will allow collaboration to take place online. The affinity networks, such as *Facebook*, will allow people to link up with others electronically, and interest-based networks (e.g., online communities of practice or communities of interest) will allow people to link with others sharing similar passions and interests. Friendster.com, for example, is a site where people can link up online for dating through friend-of-friend connections. LinkedIn.com is another site for linking up people through friend-of-friend connections, this time for jobs.

As an individual's social network grows, so might his or her opportunities, whether it's the opportunity to meet new friends, apply for new jobs, learn about health-related problems, or something else. The growth of an individual's social network should have a multiplicity effect, whereby the nodes on the networks can rapidly grow through friends-of-friends connections.

WHAT ROLES DO PEOPLE PLAY IN THESE NETWORKS?

Brokering roles can be identified through applying social network analysis to an organization. One categorization of roles deals with isolates, carriers, transmitters, and receivers. "Isolates" are people who keep to themselves and are unconnected from the central networks. "Carriers" are those people who carry knowledge and cross between departments in organizations. "Transmitters" are those people who are willing to share their knowledge with others, and "receivers" are those who are willing to receive knowledge from others. If an organization, for example, has more isolates than transmitters and receivers, then this organization probably doesn't have a good knowledge-sharing culture. Likewise, if there are more receivers than transmitters, knowledge-sharing activities are probably occurring less frequently than desired, as people are willing to receive knowledge but aren't willing to transmit it to their colleagues.

Another way to classify types of people in networks, according to Rob Cross at the University of Virginia, is as central connectors, boundary spanners, peripheral specialists, and information brokers (www.net

workroundtable.org) "Central connectors" are those who have a high degree of centrality or power in the organization. That is, more people may seek advice from these individuals than from others in the organization. The "boundary spanners" are those individuals who collaborate across departments or groups in the organization. "Information brokers" are those who are primarily sharing knowledge within a given department and may also have indirect connections to people. "Peripheral specialists" are those who are relatively isolated from others or on the periphery of the network. These people could be newcomers to the organization, who haven't yet built up their network, or an expert, for example, in the IT area or in a specialized research area who may work somewhat alone and be isolated from the central network.

Some people in a network act as facilitators. Their role is primarily to advise and put individuals in contact with others. They may possess a high degree of relationship knowledge, that is, they know who to go to for answers in an organizational setting. This "who knows whom" knowledge can be as important as, or even paramount to, some strategic or expert knowledge. Others in a network may serve as the central attractor—in much the same way that a good-looking person may attract the attention of others in a room, this person will attract others because of his or her resources or knowledge. And there are still others who may have the "leave me alone" attitude; they are most comfortable working by themselves or with a very small network of folks.

WHAT'S AHEAD?

In the following chapters, we explore the various brokering roles in organizations and how social network analysis can identify knowledge flows and gaps. We also see how social networking can be linked with innovation, and we examine the issue of trust in developing social networks. In the end, the reader should be better able to develop social networks and apply social network analysis to help create a knowledge-management strategy for an organization. Social networks as a topic is gaining worldwide interest of late, and as organizations develop their human capital, workforce development, and succession planning strategies, social networking will be a key component.

2

LINKING SOCIAL
NETWORKING TO INNOVATION

Social networks are critical for the generation of knowledge, and hence, innovation. According to Debra Amidon (1999), "knowledge innovation" is "the creation, evolution, exchange, and application of new ideas into marketable goods and services." Social networks can stimulate knowledge flows and serve as incubators for new ideas for marketable goods and services. Discussing one's thoughts with others, combining one's ideas with those of collaborators, and internalizing one's own thoughts can facilitate the knowledge-creation process. Social networks can play a powerful part in the process of synergizing one's ideas with those of others, and improve the process of knowledge exchanges and the generation of new ideas.

Let's take a look at the innovation process to see how social networking plays a role. The first component of the process is research, to see what others have done in a given area. Once an understanding is gained of the current state of the art, the second step involves postulation, whereby an individual or group may brainstorm or apply other creativity-enhancing techniques in order to pose new ideas. Once some ideas are generated, the third step is applying analogical reasoning to see if a new idea can be adapted from an existing one—much as case-based reasoning is used in problem solving to see if a target solution can be applied or adapted from an existing base solution. The fourth step deals with verification and research to see if this new idea, approach, product, or service has been offered before (coming back to the first step). If it has not, the last step could be jubilation, or a sense of eureka from generating a new idea (i.e., innovation) that has been considered for technical, economic, marketing, and operational feasibility. Certainly, social networks can play a role in the second step (postulation) as new ideas can be generated through one's social network.

In Jonathon Cummings' online course titled "Managing the Innovation Process," offered on the Massachusetts Institute of Technology website (ocw.mit.edu/OcwWeb/Sloan-School-of-Management/15-351Managing the-Innovation-ProcessFall2002/CourseHome), Cummings states that (1) innovation can arise through structural holes; (2) innovation is transferred through informal networks; and (3) innovation often requires changes in social structures. From these conclusions, a direct link can be made between innovation and social networking.

In his first conclusion, Cummings refers to "structural holes." Social networking analysis can be used to identify such holes. For example, SNA might reveal that one department in an organization that should be part of a key knowledge flow doesn't appear to be either receiving or transmitting this knowledge. This department would be a structural hole in terms of this particular type of knowledge. However, even though a structural hole may exist, innovation can still develop if the intraorganizational knowledge flows are fluid and people within the department (versus across departments) are well connected. (When everyone is connected to everyone else in the department, "density" is said to be 100 percent.) Thus, almost in isolation, innovation can still surface from structural holes; however, innovation is more likely to occur when structural holes do not exist.

Cummings also indicates that innovation is transferred through informal networks. This is the "grapevine" (watercooler) effect that has proven to work well in many organizations. Cummings' last point—the need for change in the social structure of most organizations in order to foster innovation—is particularly relevant to knowledge-management principles. A basic component of knowledge management (that is, leveraging knowledge internally and externally) is building and nurturing a knowledge-sharing culture. In an innovative environment, there will be risks, and a lessons-learned/best-practice environment should be instilled throughout the organization, so that the organization can learn from its successes and its failures. A culture that allows people to try new ideas, even though some may fail, is central in fostering an innovative organizational environment. An innovative environment is accepting of risk, and a risk-adverse culture may need some change agents to foster a more innovative mindset. This type of innovating culture, or social structure, may be quite different from the status quo of an organization.

In the March 6, 2006, issue of *Business Week*, the results of a 2005 survey by Development Dimensions International were reported. In this survey, 4,559 corporate managers in thirty-six industries were asked to consider the leadership qualities they respected most in executives. An interesting outcome was that in the United States, only 4 percent of the managers surveyed selected creativity/innovation as one of the most highly respected qualities, while in China, 16 percent cited it. In the United States, the "ability to bring in the numbers" was the top respected leadership quality (with 36 percent of managers selecting it). Despite management's concentration on innovation, it appears that U.S. executives say their companies don't rate innovation as highly as they should in terms of being a highly respected leadership quality among executives.

REMOVING THE "I" IN INNOVATION

Social networks can enhance collaboration and teamwork as they increase intra- and interdepartmental organizational knowledge flows. Social networks help remove the "I" from innovation, and focus on the "we" or collaborative element to generate creative, innovative ideas. Through social networks, collaboration can be further fostered to create knowledge.

IDEO (www.ideo.com) is a company that helps other organizations innovate. In talking about what he terms "the ten faces of innovation," Tom Kelley, general manager of IDEO, discusses three categories of personas (www.tenfacesofinnovation.com/tenfaces/index.htm). The "learning personas" are the learning roles that people should adopt in order to not be complacent. "Organizing personas" are the organizing roles, and include such types as the "hurdler" (someone who tries new things and gets around obstacles), the "collaborator" (who breaks down functional silos), and the "director" (a "big picture" person). The best ideas must continuously compete for time, attention, and resources. The other category of personas is "building personas." In these roles, individuals use insights learned from the learning personas and directed through the organizing personas to cause innovation to occur.

Social networking plays a role in each of these three categories of personas. The "cross-pollinator," one of Kelley's learning personas, certainly is a "social networker." The cross-pollinator tries to make associative links wherever possible. The "collaborator," one of the building personas, applies social-networking principles and tries to integrate people and thoughts across organizational stovepipes. And the "storyteller," one of the building personas, applies social-networking and knowledge-management techniques to improve the sharing and transfer of knowledge.

Certainly, innovation can be achieved in isolation (such as in a structural hole), but it typically develops through a collaborative exchange of ideas. Knowledge transfer and assimilation foster innovation. Social networking can be a mechanism for knowledge exchange and can facilitate the knowledge-sharing process.

More and more, organizations are expanding their knowledge networks in creative ways. Online communities of practice are used to exchange thoughts and information and help to enlarge one's social network. Hallmark, for example, has online communities that allow it to reach out to its customers. Through these communities, customers can, for example, suggest new ideas for greeting cards and other products. DaimlerChrysler has established "tech clubs" to stimulate new ideas relating to their automobile's subsystems. NASA's Academy of Program/Project Engineering Leadership offers knowledge-sharing forums where seasoned project managers meet with up-and-coming project leaders and exchange stories on successes and failures. This discussion helps newer project leaders apply lessons learned so that the wheel isn't reinvented and can lead to the generation of new ideas.

When it comes to innovation, some people may exhibit more of a knowledge-hoarding mentality than a knowledge-sharing perspective. Scientists, even though they typically work in teams, still have the "I" view in terms of being the first author and the main one credited for a particular discovery. Engineers, on the other hand, exhibit perhaps more collaborative (versus competitive) instincts, as they typically work in project teams and believe that the whole is greater than the sum of its parts. The disciplines and cultural attitudes can affect an individual's knowledge-sharing behavior, and could ultimately lead to barriers for knowledge sharing and knowledge creation. Knowledge-sharing behaviors can be studied by applying the theory of reasoned action, wherein attitudes are predicted by evaluating an indivual's intention to perform certain behaviors and the available subjective norms. As we will see in the coming chapters, the use of social network analysis can be utilized to map knowledge flows and gaps to further study knowledge-sharing patterns.

PARADIGM SHIFTS NEEDED FOR KNOWLEDGE SHARING

As was suggested above, a paradigm shift is needed to encourage knowledge sharing and improved social networking. In the United States, the elementary and middle school education typically involves group work and team-building experiences. A multidisciplinary look at the studies is usually conducted, with integration across school subjects. However, as the individual enters high school and certainly college and beyond, the collectivistic approach is subsumed by the individualistic perspective. For example, in college, there are separate courses on biology, chemistry, physics, and the like. A more integrative approach might be topic- or inquiry-based instruction. Both of these approaches incorporate the various disciplines as they are related to the issue or topic. Various biological, chemical, environmental, and public policy related information could be discussed when studying an oil spill, for example. This integrated type of teaching encourages the development of problem solvers in a group, synergistic manner. It encourages knowledge sharing (versus knowledge hoarding) to take place.

A paradigm shift in our educational process is necessary to facilitate and develop knowledge-sharing principles. When these principles are established, social networking can be maximized. The College of Integrated Science and Technology at James Madison University in Harrisonburg, Virginia, is one of the few colleges that focuses on this integrated approach. There are about one thousand undergraduates majoring in integrated science and technology at the college. The School of Informatics at Indiana University also encourages an integrated approach to teaching.

One of my colleagues defines "cheating" as the failure to help someone in a time of need. This is a fundamentally different way of thinking, as we typically define cheating as, for example, helping someone during an examination when it is against the rules. The issue of knowledge hoarding versus knowledge sharing is at play here. For those who believe that "sharing knowledge is power," then perhaps "cheating" should take on a definition more like the one adopted by my colleague. Of course, this runs greatly counter to the traditional establishment, but perhaps this may be one way of being socially responsible and making the world a better place, so to speak. This is an interesting concept, worthy of further investigation.

Knowledge-management techniques can facilitate knowledge sharing and development of social networks. Knowledge management deals with how best to leverage knowledge internally and externally. Through web-based and intranet technologies, we can now connect isolated islands of knowledge, forming bridges between these islands to form connections. Two main approaches are usually used in knowledge management: codification and personalization. Codification deals with the "collection" approach, wherein tacit knowledge is codified in some form in order to make it easily accessed and shared. Codification is normally systems oriented. Examples include lessons-learned/best-practice systems, online searchable multimedia asset management systems, knowledge repositories, and the like. Personalization is a "connection" approach, which accentuates the people-to-people connections. Online communities of practice, expertise-locator systems, knowledge-sharing forums, knowledge fairs, mentoring programs, job rotation and shadowing, and other knowledge-sharing approaches are examples of the personalization method.

The company Accenture uses a system it calls Knowledge Xchange as its knowledge-transfer system. This system uses hybrid forms of both codification and personalization. Lessons learned, key documents, online communities, expertise locators, data-mining techniques, and other approaches are contained within Accenture's Knowledge Xchange. This codification-personalization system allows Accenture to share knowledge and expertise among its seventy-five thousand employees in forty-seven countries.

Where, then, is the "connection" between social networking and these knowledge-management approaches? Personalization approaches are among the most useful in helping an employee to further develop his or her social network in an organization. Through an expertise-locator system—an online "yellow pages" of expertise—for example, an individual can identify people with common interests, find people who can answer his or her questions, or locate collaborators for a project management team. Certainly, online communities can greatly facilitate the sharing of information and knowledge with others, hence building shared values and further developing an individual's social network. The hope is that through developing these social networks, knowledge sharing will be enhanced and lead to knowledge creation and innovation.

Improved knowledge-sharing processes and larger social networks can help individuals find answers to questions more easily and quickly. Understanding that SNA can help organizations improve these internal knowledge-sharing processes, specialized companies are being developed that will perform SNA collaboration services for clients. One such company is IBM On Demand Innovation Services (ODIS), a partnership between IBM Research and IBM Business Consulting Services. IBM Research applied SNA internally to study communication and collaboration patterns among their summer interns. The results certainly have the potential of improving innovation and productivity within the organization:

> In one engagement, IBM Research used SNA to conduct a study of 15 summer interns, their mentors, and other members of the group. The goal was to see how quickly the interns could make the human connections necessary to accomplish an assigned task. Researchers found that the interns lacked knowledge about people's roles and expertise in the group. As a result, the interns tended to seek information from other people less frequently than did permanent employees, and often had to query several people to get their answers. The analysis also showed that the interns' impressions about the company as a good place to work depended largely on whether they knew who to ask for information and whether their questions were answered in a timely fashion. These results confirmed other

published studies showing that awareness is integral to successful on-boarding and productivity. In this case, SNA helped identify and address ways to make the internship program more effective for the future, in particular building awareness and access. Recommendations included giving interns and mentors a chance to discuss expectations at the beginning, encouraging the interns to be more proactive about seeking help, and focusing on what roles people play in the organization as part of the orientation process. (domino.research.ibm.com/odis/odis.nsf/pages/solution.13.html)

LINKING SOCIAL NETWORKING TO HUMAN CAPITAL STRATEGY

Through social networking, an organization's human capital strategy can be enhanced in a number of ways. First, as we move towards a more flexible workforce, social networking allows a single individual's knowledge to be more broadly shared among the individual's community members. This will provide some level of redundancy in the case of the individual retiring or moving to a new organization. It will also help avoid "single points of failure" in terms of expertise. It is important to apply appropriate safeguards to be certain that backups are in place, especially in terms of critical "at risk" knowledge. Social networking can reduce the reliance on a single individual as knowledge is more readily available.

Second, a social network can bridge knowledge and skills gaps. For example, a social network can be used to tap into a pool of expertise that may be unconnected from the organization. It may be more difficult to identify or contact some external experts if they are not linked with a social network in some particular area of specialization or interest. Last, social networking can facilitate plugging the knowledge gaps in organizations created by structural holes in the flow of knowledge through the organization.

Four key pillars should underpin the development of an organization's human capital strategy. They are knowledge management, competency management, performance management, and change management. Knowledge management, as we have been discussing, allows knowledge to be retained, shared, and disseminated internally and externally (where appropriate). Competency management deals with determining what competencies are needed to produce the organization's workforce of the future. Performance management involves recognizing and rewarding people for their performance, or providing negative incentives for lack of performance. Change management deals with putting change-management processes in place in order to build and nurture a knowledge-sharing culture.

Social networking has its closest link with knowledge management as part of the human capital strategy. In terms of knowledge management, where we look at knowledge flows and gaps as part of a knowledge audit, there are four main types of intellectual capital that organizations should embrace: human capital, structural capital, relationship capital, and competitor capital. "Human capital" refers to the brainpower that employees have and how best to capture and leverage this tacit knowledge. "Structural capital" refers to intangibles that you can't easily bring home with you from the office, like intellectual property rights or certain databases perhaps. "Relationship capital" refers to the knowledge that an individual can glean from customers or stakeholders to feed back into the organization. "Competitor capital" is the knowledge learned from the organization's competition and how best to apply this knowledge to make one's own organization more competitive in the marketplace. Through SNA, knowledge flows and gaps in the organization can be identified in order to increase the value of all four types of intellectual capital.

One human capital strategy that organizations are applying more frequently is to bring back retirees part-time in various knowledge-sharing roles. In addition, formal phased retirement programs are becoming more common in companies. In these programs, the number of hours an individual works is reduced as the individual nears retirement age, which allows and encourages the individual to become more active in passing on his or her knowledge to his or her successors. Retirees can be used for mentoring purposes, in knowledge-sharing forums to apply their organizational narratives on what worked and what didn't (and why), in knowledge-retention efforts to build the institutional memory of the organization, in part-time project team consulting roles, in facilitator/moderator's roles in online communities, and given other responsibilities to fill knowledge and skills gaps. Of course, these types of knowledge-sharing activities should lead to building more knowledgeable social networks in order for the organization to become more productive and responsive to market needs.

THE "I" IN INTRAPRENEURSHIP

Innovation can take place internally and externally. Many people focus on entrepreneurship, but intrapreneurship—the creation of innovative ideas within organizations—can be just as valuable. Intrapreneurship can be evidenced in employees developing new ways to improve internal processes or creating new approaches to improve communications within an organization. Social networking can foster intrapreneurship and the resulting innovation. Linking people in the organization and allowing them to share and exchange knowledge facilitates intrapreneurship. Connecting people, along with their collection of knowledge bases, can provide ample fodder to nourish the intrapreneurship appetite.

As far back as 1985, John Naisbitt and Patricia Aburdene, in their book *Re-inventing the Corporation*, stressed that intrapreneurship needs to be applied to generate new products and services for businesses. Some corporations have employee contests to encourage intrapreneurship. These contests might reward employees for creating the best new idea for improving worker productivity, for an idea that will increase customer satisfaction, or for generating an innovative product design. A number of corporations provide seed money to finance intrapreneurial ideas. The manufacturer of Post-It Notes, 3M, has been a leader for pushing an intrapreneurial spirit among its employees.

In the coming years, as companies try to cope with increasing competition, quick ways to stimulate intrapreneurship, as well as entrepreneurship, will be needed. Social networking may be one way to create the interactions among employees necessary for developing a marketplace of ideas. In the years ahead, as senior management's time horizons shorten, being able to connect people to more rapidly generate new ideas that have great business value will be an invaluable trait to possess within an organization.

3

STRATEGIC INTELLIGENCE: THE SYNERGY OF KNOWLEDGE MANAGEMENT, BUSINESS INTELLIGENCE, AND COMPETITIVE INTELLIGENCE

In the previous chapters, we discussed how social networking leads to innovation and improved knowledge flows among employees and between employees and customers. Social networking can also lead to another vitally important component in organizations, namely strategic intelligence. In this chapter, we discuss strategic intelligence and the role of social networks in increasing the strategic intelligence in an organization.

"Strategic intelligence" is usually defined in terms of the information necessary to formulate defense or national policy. However, when we talk of strategic intelligence in a business context, we are not discussing intelligence as it would be understood from a military or defense perspective. Rather, we are interested in strategic intelligence in terms of improving an organization's strategic decision-making ability. Certainly, strategic intelligence has been applied and continues to be used in defense environments, but our focus will be on creating and utilizing strategic intelligence from the synergy of three main areas: knowledge management, business intelligence, and competitive intelligence.

KNOWLEDGE MANAGEMENT

Knowledge management may form the inner core of the strategic intelligence onion. As mentioned in the previous chapter, knowledge management deals with creating value from an organization's intangible assets—namely, the human capital, structural capital, relationship capital, and competitor capital. Human capital refers to the brainpower of an organization's employees, and how best to capture, leverage, and make available the tacit knowledge that resides in the heads of the employees. Structural capital deals with knowledge that an individual can't easily take home from the office, like intellectual property rights. Relationship capital, also referred to as social or customer capital, is knowledge that is learned from the customers and stakeholders and then fed back into the organization. The last and newest type of capital is competitor capital. This is the knowledge learned about an organization's competitors and how best to share and leverage this knowledge towards improving the innovation process.

Knowledge management (KM) typically involves four key processes: knowledge identification and capture, knowledge sharing, knowledge application, and knowledge creation. Critical "at risk" knowledge in an organization is identified and captured, then this knowledge is shared, combined with other knowledge, internalized and applied, and new knowledge is hopefully created. Most organizations use knowledge management to increase innovation, organize their corporate knowledge, build the institutional memory of the organization, improve the sense of belonging and community in the organization, and stimulate worker productivity. Many organizations have used knowledge-management efforts successfully; when these efforts have failed, it has been due mostly to the misalignment of the KM strategy with the organization's strategic/business mission and vision. Additionally, if the KM plan is poorly designed, then knowledge management may not be effective.

BUSINESS INTELLIGENCE

Business intelligence (BI) deals with internal information and knowledge within the organization. Data warehousing, data mining, and knowledge repositories are all elements of business intelligence. At the Knowledge Management and Business Intelligence Workshop held in April 2005 in Germany, business intelligence was defined as "an active, model-based and prospective approach to discover and explain hidden, decision-relevant aspects in large amounts of business data to better inform business decision processes" (wm2005.iese.fraunhofer.de). At the Gartner Group's Business Intelligence Summit held in March 2005 in Chicago, the push was for organizations to concentrate on formulating enterprise-wide BI strategies and applying best practices. Many organizations have been focusing on the skills and planning issues relating to successful BI implementations.

Knowledge management can facilitate BI strategy. For example, in applying BI best practices, knowledge management also encourages learning from previous successes and failures (e.g., lessons-learned/best-practice systems). Knowledge management can enhance the BI process through its emphasis on knowledge elicitation and sharing techniques (e.g., business rules). As BI and competitive intelligence (CI) evolve, an understanding of the various links between entities and knowledge sources becomes important (e.g., social network analysis, knowledge maps, knowledge audits, and discovery informatics).

COMPETITIVE INTELLIGENCE

The third vital component of strategic intelligence is competitive intelligence (CI). According to the Society of Competitive Intelligence Professionals (SCIP), CI is a systematic process for collecting, analyzing, and managing external information and knowledge to improve an organization's decision-making process (www.scip.org). The strict focus here, unlike in BI and much of KM, is the external knowledge that is learned from the competition and channeled back into the organization's knowledge base. Some people say that KM is looking down the hallway from your office and CI is looking out your office window.

Competitive intelligence professionals spend a lot of time and effort in the intelligence collection phase. Collecting CI, through primary and secondary research methods, is critical and necessary. The analysis of this collected information and knowledge is equally as important as the collection of the information. Typically, though, the CI professional spends almost twice as much time collecting the information as he or she does analyzing it. Hopefully, as SCIP starts a certification program and with graduate certificates in competitive intelligence available (as through the program at Johns Hopkins University; see business.jhu.edu), the CI professional will be able to spend the necessary time and possess the requisite skills and techniques to analyze the collected information. All organizations should be engaged in collecting and analyzing CI. Oftentimes, the strategy, business and product development, research and development, strategic and competitive analysis, marketing, and other departments are charged with obtaining and analyzing CI. According to the 2003–2004 SCIP CI Professionals Survey Salary Report (www.scip.org), the Washington, D.C.–Baltimore area has the eighth highest concentration of CI professionals (www.scip.org). These individuals are from the following major industries: biotechnology, telecom, IT, consulting, utilities/energy, financial/real estate, manufacturing, hotel, insurance, and government/defense.

STRATEGIC INTELLIGENCE

Strategic intelligence is the synergy of knowledge management, business intelligence, and competitive intelligence as applied towards improving the strategic decision-making process of the organization. Unfortunately, the KM, BI, and CI communities each grew fairly independently; each field has its unique best features. In the past few years, these three communities have started to merge, as evidenced by enterprise content management systems with increased "intelligence" (via business rules) and sophistication. In spite of this blending, there is still tremendous opportunity for growth in order to take advantage of the complementary features that each field has to offer. This synergy should be targeted towards the strategic decision making of the organization, defined as strategic intelligence. Let's now see how social networking fits into strategic intelligence.

SOCIAL NETWORKING AND
STRATEGIC INTELLIGENCE

In a study on knowledge sharing among research and development (R&D) scientists, Ensign and Hebert (2004) found that past behavior and expected action influence knowledge-sharing decisions. These factors are dimensions of reputation. They also found that the level of knowledge flow to the source relative to the knowledge flow from the source, versus the frequency of interaction, plays a key role in the decision to disseminate technological knowledge. Additionally, they found that geographic factors (such as, the physical distance between scientists) play a major role in a scientist's decision to share knowledge with an R&D colleague in the same organization.

In their study on co-located social networks, Farnham et al. (2004) found that e-mails and mailing lists were used as much as phone conversations to plan social activities, and that said usage was positively correlated with measures of friendship satisfaction, sense of community, and percentage of time spent socializing. Awazu (2004) has examined the roles of informal network players in how knowledge is shared.

As evidenced in the various research and other work, social networks do have a role to play in knowledge sharing, but various conditions have to be met. As stated above, Ensign and Hebert's research (2004) indicates that past behavior and expected action are critical parts of the knowledge-transfer formula. Both the ability and openness to reciprocate on the part of a potential knowledge recipient, and previous knowledge-sharing behavior have an effect on whether a knowledge holder is willing to share his or her knowledge with a potential recipient. The underlying factor is interpersonal trust, and whether people have bonded well enough and feel secure to share their knowledge.

Farnham et al.'s work (2004) suggests that electronic means can provide an experience that builds a sense of community similar to that provided by face-to-face encounters. Social networking, through online communities of practice and in-person connections, can aid towards improving an individual's productivity as a stronger sense of employee morale is created. As individual productivity improves, new ideas might be created, which can then be transformed into improving the organizational intelligence. At the strategic level, this organizational intelligence might be called "strategic intelligence," in terms of its ability to enhance the organization's strategic decision making.

BLOGS AND WIKIS AS FORMS OF SOCIAL NETWORKING FOR CREATING INTELLIGENCE

Blogs and wikis are great forms of social networking that can help in knowledge transfer and knowledge creation. According to Wikipedia, a blog is a website in which items are posted on a regular basis and displayed in reverse chronological order (en.wikipedia.org). Here is an example of a blog dealing with social networking:

> Dennis Wood (director of human capital for vSpring) has a great article in the recent *Connect* magazine about executive recruiting and hiring right.
>
> Dennis is a star. He is the most LinkedIn person in Utah (he passed me a long time ago) and in his article he discusses how he recently used LinkedIn to land a CTO for a vSpring portfolio company.
>
> I remember a year or year and a half ago trying for a full hour over lunch to convince Paul . . . about the value of LinkedIn.com. He remained stubbornly unconvinced. So now it is great to see his own human capital director endorsing it for all startup companies as a great way to recruit!
>
> I have also been unsuccessful most of the time in convincing CEOs and VCs to start blogging.
>
> The social networking value of a blog is extremely high. I get contacts nearly every week from smart people around that [*sic*] world that comment on my blog or email [*sic*] me directly. Most of our Provo Labs job applicants come from people who read our blogs and feel a connection to the way we think and to what we are doing.
>
> So Dennis, if you're reading, please start a vSpring human capital blog, then write a [*sic*] article about how your blog is attracting great talent to your portfolio companies. And vindicate me yet again! (Paul's entry dated February 17, 2006, at www.infobaseventures.com/blog/categories/social-networking-watch)

Wikis can be also be used to develop knowledge-sharing networks. A wiki system, according to Wikipedia, provides various tools that allow the user community to easily monitor the constantly changing wiki entries and discuss the issues that emerge in trying to achieve a general consensus about wiki content. Wikis allow for "open editing" so that both the organization and content of contributions can be edited.

Blogs and wikis encourage group communication and knowledge sharing. This should hopefully lead to innovation. In his book *The Art of Innovation*, Tom Kelley talks about innovation as a very goal-oriented process; but under time deadlines, groups tend to focus on end results. Kelley feels that the innovation process should focus on verbs, not nouns. For example, the goal should be to create not a more beautiful store, but rather a better shopping experience. Further, the journey should be a learning experience, rather than just a means to a destination point. In a knowledge-sharing context, the fun part may be the exchange of ideas and bouncing thoughts off each other. The interaction of the group discussion may be the stimulating part of the knowledge exchange, versus the end message that results.

SOCIAL NETWORKING INFLUENCING STRATEGIC INTELLIGENCE DEVELOPMENT: AN EXAMPLE

Social networking suggests that the whole is greater than the sum of its parts. This synergy can be shown in the use of teamwork versus separate individual efforts. Let's look at the transcript I wrote for a video clip about project planning. I call it "Avoiding Being a Political Football."

Process Based Mission Assurance
March 14, 2006, 12:31:08

I'm Jay Liebowitz, the Knowledge Management Officer at NASA Goddard, and I have a story about avoiding being the political football, and hopefully, you'll enjoy this. I was involved with a project where there were two teams of individuals who, it turned out, were doing the same, exact work. And I didn't realize that was going to happen until I was doing my data collection effort, and discovered that there was simply another team who was tasked to do the exact work that I was. I started to probe and wondered why that would be so, being a duplication of effort and resources. And, it turned out, management felt that the other team didn't have credibility because they lacked the technical subject matter expertise that was needed to conduct the study. However, I didn't have the domain knowledge which was necessary for properly carrying on the study. So, instead of trying to fight against the other team and be caught in the middle of this political football field, I decided to join forces with the other team, and it worked out extremely well. They were able to get the technical expertise necessary to do the work; I was able to get the complementary domain knowledge to carry out the work, and, the bottom line was that the study that we both produced had very good reviews. Management decided to follow those recommendations, and everyone was a winner. So, that was a nice way of trying to avoid being caught in the middle.

This type of occurrence could happen at any time, but it's probably most likely to happen in the project formulation stage. So as you're putting together the teams and looking at various talents, you always want to make sure you have a complementary set of skills and also be very careful of some of the political nature of how people interact and the organizational dynamics. So, I think this is really critical—especially at the beginning stages—and hopefully, these types of activities will be useful throughout the project development phase. (pbma.hq.nasa.gov/index.php?interview with=117&interviewtitle=&interviewtranscript=&btnsubmit=search&complex=0&fuseaction=videolibrary.results)

This example has two teams first pitted against each other, but through early acknowledgment of this situation, the two teams merge into one to produce a winning team. By collaborating together, synergy resulted in a whole stronger than individual parts. In much the same way, social networking has a related effect whereby the group interactions and network connections made can lead to revelations and good decisions.

In this example, the strategic intelligence dealt with how to build a ground control center in a faster and less costly manner than what had been done previously. The business intelligence component was applying lessons learned from previous satellite missions in terms of designing ground systems and control centers. The knowledge management element dealt with applying artificial intelligence techniques to leverage the knowledge of control center design experts. The competitive intelligence component was to compare what other satellite missions had done and what future similar missions were planning to do in terms of their control center design. By finding the intersection of these three elements, strategic intelligence can result to determine a "faster, cheaper, and better" approach to doing satellite control center design.

SOCIAL NETWORKING ROLES IN PRODUCING STRATEGIC INTELLIGENCE

Through social networking analysis, we can identify certain types of brokering roles that individuals play in a given network. The "central connector" is the individual who people come to often for advice. The "liaison" is the individual who spans between two groups. The "peripheral specialist" is the individual who is "outside" (i.e., on the periphery) of the network and is often isolated and unconnected from the network. Each of these brokering roles can be influential in the development, application, and management of strategic intelligence.

The central connector can work in an individual's favor or not. For example, the central connector can be the carrier of information and knowledge, allowing the knowledge flows to be fluid. Or, on the contrary, the central connector could cause a bottleneck if he or she desires. This would inhibit the knowledge-sharing process. In promoting strategic intelligence, a central connector could play an important role as he or she is typically at the hub of social network interactions and could greatly facilitate the development and dissemination of the strategic intelligence.

The liaison can be someone who links his or her group with another group in the organization, or an individual who links two groups separate from his or her own. This person may have a fair amount of relationship knowledge, knowing "who knows whom" to help produce and disseminate strategic intelligence. This person is a "networker" who can build the tentacles of social links to quickly spread information.

The peripheral specialist is often a newcomer to the organization or an expert in a particular field. The neophyte hasn't been able to develop his or her social network, as he or she is new to the organization.

The expert may be a particular scientist or individual who can do his or her work without interacting with many others. The IT (information technology) or computer guru may be this type of person. However, it is becoming harder to find these peripheral specialists in organizations because almost everyone has a social network of one kind or another. Even if you have a well-known researcher in the R&D department of an organization, that individual can't really work in isolation. He or she needs to connect with marketing and sales to better understand the customer's requirements, which is necessary if he or she is to develop new products that the customer will want to buy. Further, the R&D folks need to let the sales and marketing departments know what new products are coming down the line so they can be marketed appropriately. Thus, the peripheral specialist, even though somewhat isolated, still can contribute to strategic intelligence.

The next chapter will discuss social network analysis and how knowledge flows and brokering roles can be determined.

4

SOCIAL NETWORK ANALYSIS:
AN INTRODUCTION

Social network analysis (SNA) can be used to map relationships and knowledge flows between individuals, departments, or other entities. It is useful in both locating and developing social networks. Social network analysis grew out of Harvard in the 1920s, and has its roots in sociology and education. Since its inception, SNA has been applied in a range of cases, from determining knowledge-sharing behaviors and patterns of physicians to analyzing collaboration flows between senior executives of newly merged multinational corporations.

Through SNA, a mapping of relationships between actors/nodes can be developed. In figure 4.1, the circular diagram represents employee interactions in an organization. Links or arcs depict the strength of the relationships between the actors/nodes. In this figure, there are 698 employees on the periphery of the circle with corresponding connections that indicate advice-seeking behaviors. Part of the circle has no connections because 225 employees indicated they sought knowledge from 473 others who were not surveyed. The thicker concentrations of lines emanating to employees shows the employees most sought after for work-related advice.

Let's step back from SNA for a moment to discuss the concept of "knowledge audits." In knowledge-management parlance, a "knowledge

Figure 4.1. Employee Advice-Seeking Interactions

audit" is conducted to provide a baseline that an organization can use to determine knowledge-sharing practices, knowledge flows, and knowledge resources within the organization. This baseline is essential for crafting an effective knowledge-management strategy for the organization. As part of a knowledge audit, SNA is useful for identifying knowledge flows in order to determine the informal social networks in the organization. At the same time, SNA can identify structural holes in the organization whereby certain departments, for example, may be unconnected from others in the various flows of knowledge. If the strategic planning department is revealed to be a structural hole in the flow of strategic knowledge throughout the organization, then this may signal a lack of credibility on the part of the department. If the communications department is on the periphery of the network, instead of being at the hub, then perhaps it may need to be repositioned within the organization for improved effectiveness and knowledge transfer. (Structural holes are discussed in more detail in chapter 2.)

As discussed briefly in chapter 3, SNA can provide insights into the various brokering roles individuals assume in an organization. "Isolates" may be on the periphery or outside of the social network. These individuals may be newcomers to the organization who haven't had a chance to build their social network yet. "Periphery specialists" also often play the role of isolates; that is, certain peripheral experts may not need to interact heavily with others and function as isolates. Another brokering role is the "carrier." This is an individual who crosses between two or more groups or departments in the organization. This individual may be thought of as a boundary spanner. Another brokering role is that of "transmitter." The transmitter is willing to transmit or share his or her knowledge with others. A last role is the "receiver," someone who is willing to receive and accept someone else's knowledge.

By examining the composite of the individuals who assume these different brokering roles, one can paint a picture about the organization as a whole. For example, if there is a disproportionate number of isolates and carriers in an organization, compared with transmitters and receivers, then the organization's social network may be quite shallow and fragmented. Some organizations say that they don't have a knowledge "sharing" problem, they have a knowledge "asking" problem." People may be willing to share their knowledge in this case, but they are perhaps shy about asking for someone else's advice or guidance.

Let's now look at some of the basics of SNA.

COMMUNICATION MEASURES

Cross and Parker (2004) break SNA into six steps:

1. Identify a strategically important group
2. Assess meaningful and actionable relationships
3. Visually analyze the results
4. Quantitatively analyze the results
5. Create meaningful feedback sessions
6. Assess progress and effectiveness

There are various techniques that can be used to collect the data as part of the SNA, and how the techniques are applied depends on how the "strategically important group" is delineated. Surveys and follow-up interviews are among the most common ways of determining "who knows whom" and "who knows what" within an organization. One approach is to send a copy of the survey to everyone in the organization under study, and to consider the entire organization as the group under study. Another approach is to start with a select number of individuals, find out who they go to for information and knowledge, and then go to those indicated persons and ask them who they seek out. This is a "snowball approach" to delineating the "strategically important group"; the main problem with it is that the researcher may be leaving out people who should also be part of the study. A group or bounded network approach can also be used, whereby the researcher decides all the group members he or she will study and then he or she collects and analyzes relationship data between just those individuals.

The personal or egocentric approach is to ask a person to identify other people who are important for a particular task and then ask them to answer questions regarding each of these people (Cross and Parker, 2004).

Individual and group measures exist to help determine the types of relationships between actors/entities. Some of the more common individual measures are in-degree centrality, out-degree centrality, betweenness, closeness, and brokering roles. "In-degree centrality" refers to incoming ties, that is, an individual with in-degree centrality is one whom others seek out. "Out-degree centrality" refers to outgoing ties; a person with out-degree centrality is the one whom the individual being studied seeks out. "Betweenness" refers to the degree to which people act as the intermediary between two nodes. "Closeness" measures is the degree where people are at short distances (i.e., close) to others. For example, the assistant to the president would have a high degree of closeness in terms of his or her access to the president. Brokering roles (isolates, transmitters, receivers, and carriers) can also be determined as mentioned earlier in the chapter. Some of the more common group measures are density and cohesion. "Density" refers to how well connected everyone is to everyone else in the organization or group under study. For example, as mentioned earlier, density would be 100 percent if everyone were connected to everyone else in the organization or group. "Cohesion" refers to the average of the shortest paths between each pair of individuals. A form of cohesion is cliques. As the name implies, cliques refer to friends of friends or subgroups.

To help with the quantitative analysis and visualization, SNA software should be used. Two popular SNA tools are NetMiner (www.netminer. com) and UCINET/Netdraw (www.analytictech.com/Netdraw/netdraw. htm). On their website, the International Network for Social Network Analysis (INSNA, at www.insna.org) lists other SNA software that may be useful as well.

Social network analysis, via the mapping software Netdraw and UCINET 6, was used to develop the knowledge maps shown in figures 4.2 through 4.4. The first two social networks in figures 4.2 and 4.3 track the survey responses to the top two individuals in the organization whom people in the organization go to when they have questions or seek general advice. From these knowledge maps, it is easy to view key individuals (such as Kevin S., Peter B., R. Fossi, and others) whose knowledge is sought with respect to providing "general advice." The size of the nodes is proportional to their betweenness and centrality. The larger the node, the more power the individual has, because it means more people depend on that individual to make connections with other people. The smaller, dark-colored nodes in the figures show the "isolates," who aren't connected.

In figure 4.2, groupings can also be analyzed to indicate the level of connectedness and interactions between divisions. For example, the grouping with Tina T. (node 16) indicates that all those individuals are within a particular division, and they seek help within this community. Other divisions in the organization also seem to seek help from within their own communities/divisions. Figure 4.2 also shows some gatekeepers who bridge between different communities (like Sheila M. [node 28] who is connected to two divisions). Looking at these maps, one area that could be singled out for improvement would be the interlinking among the divisions. This could be achieved by increasing the interaction between the executive office and the various divisions, and also by having communications become more interconnected and linking the various divisions. The communications division, seen on the periphery in figure 4.2, should probably have a more central role.

Figure 4.3 depicts the results of an SNA using the multidimensional scaling method, which shows the clusters of connections. Here the black nodes depict "cutpoints"—if these nodes were removed, that structure would become "unconnected." The labeled number of the node has no bearing on the importance of the node.

Social network analysis can also be used to see how the employees are interacting with each other. In figure 4.4, these interactions are

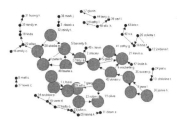

Figure 4.2. Social Network of General Advice Seeking in the Organization

Figure 4.3. Social Network of General Advice Seeking in the Organization Using Multidimensional Scaling

interpreted based upon the length of the employee's service to the organization. Figure 4.4 depicts five communities of employees: those who have been at the organization less than six months, those six months to less than one year, those one year to less than three years, those three years to less than five years, and those more than five years. The SNA shows a healthy relationship in that the employees who are the newest in the organization are seeking advice to questions from those employees who are typically fairly senior (more than five years at the organization). The organization may want to consider a mentoring program or "buddy system," however, whereby those employees who have been working less than one year can link up with those employees who have been working one to three years at the organization. This SNA reveals that currently, those working less than one year at the organization aren't generally seeking advice from their peers closest to their work experience; a mentoring program would bring these groups together and further build a sense of belonging in the organization.

Other views of SNA data are shown in figures 4.5 and 4.6. Figure 4.5 shows patterns of how individuals in the organization, blocked by de-

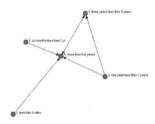

Figure 4.4. Length of Service in the Organization

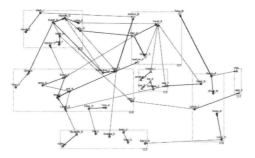

Figure 4.5. Individuals, Blocked by Departments, Seeking General Advice in the Organization

partments, seek general advice. Figure 4.6 shows a departmental view of seeking subject matter expertise in the organization. Both these figures were drawn by using NetMiner (www.netminer.com). Figure 4.6 clearly shows that the communications department is an outlier instead of being at the hub of knowledge flows.

POTENTIAL PITFALLS OF SOCIAL NETWORK ANALYSIS

With any information gathering and analyzing technique, one must be mindful of the limitations of the method. Social network analysis is no different. For example, in most research, including SNA, triangulation should be conducted so that there are three methods of collecting (and

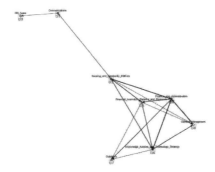

Figure 4.6. Departments Seeking Subject-Matter Expertise in the Organization

perhaps analyzing) data to ensure convergence and confidence in the data gathered. Three methods that could be used in SNA are surveys, interviews or focus groups, and ethnographic analysis/observation. Surveys might provide perceptions on advice-seeking behavior, but these perceptions may be different from what actually takes place. This is where ethnographic analysis or observation might help, allowing the researcher to actually view how interactions and advice-seeking behaviors occur. Interviews and focus groups can also delve deeper into the areas that the survey highlighted.

Another potential pitfall of SNA is the "unboundedness" of the network. For example, there may be two hundred people surveyed who indicate that they reach out to six hundred people for advice-giving and advice-seeking behavior. However, if these other four hundred people are not surveyed, then the SNA analyst may not be getting the full picture. Also, density measures will probably be very low due to the "unboundedness" of the network. This may cause some concern as the recommendations may not be "statistically significant."

A last major pitfall that is common with any survey approach is that the response rate or sample size may not be representative of the organization. One way to combat this potential problem is to have the senior leader send out an e-mail to everyone in the organization to discuss the importance of this work. This may help pave the way for more active involvement by the individuals in the organization. Additionally, providing gifts for the first x number of people who complete the survey or having middle managers strongly encourage their staff to complete the survey will also increase participation.

WHY IS SOCIAL NETWORK ANALYSIS USEFUL?

Developing a map that highlights the knowledge flows and gaps in organizations can help identify improved techniques for knowledge sharing across the organization. Social network analysis can answer such questions as these:

- How well are people communicating within departments and across departments?

- How are different types of knowledge being passed on from one person to another?
- Do the newer employees have access to the more senior ones, in order to ask questions?
- Who has the "real" versus "perceived" power in the organization, at least according to knowledge flows?
- How are the people at different levels in the organization communicating with one another at each level and throughout the management hierarchy?
- Which departments are "structural holes" and "out of the loop" in terms of the flow of particular types of knowledge?
- What types of brokering roles do various individuals and departments play in the flow of knowledge in the organization?
- How can the organization improve its communication and knowledge-sharing patterns to increase its effectiveness and efficiency?

Social network analysis should be used as part of the knowledge audit in forming a baseline for knowledge-sharing behaviors and patterns in the organization. Identifying the central connectors, gatekeepers, boundary spanners, and peripheral specialists in an organization can be a help when striving to improve an organization's structure and increase the organization's productivity. Knowledge management is typically used to integrate across functional silos in an organization. Through SNA, informal networks in the organization are identified that can help knowledge flow cross-organizationally. Social network analysis will also show which departments are considered structural holes. Perhaps a restructuring that would fill these structural holes should be implemented in order to make them more connected within the organization.

Another reason for applying SNA is to improve project teaming in the organization. Social network analysis can indicate what cross-functional teams may be most useful, and may also suggest which mentoring system may work best. Additionally, SNA can help improve communications and collaboration within the organization to get people better connected and informed as to what's happening in the organization.

Through SNA, a knowledge-management strategy can be created to increase knowledge creation in the organization. When people are better connected, ideas can be more easily shared which in turn will hopefully lead to new thoughts and innovation. Also, employee morale should improve as a sense of belonging and community should be fostered by cross-teaming, cross-departmental staff meetings, mentoring programs, knowledge sharing forums, and the like.

GETTING STARTED IN SOCIAL NETWORK ANALYSIS

This book and others in social networking will provide some initial background in SNA. The International Network for Social Network Analysis (INSNA, at www.insna.org) is also a rich resource. Members of INSNA have access to the online *Journal of Social Structure*, can attend the annual International Sunbelt Social Network Conference, and are part of a community of social network analysts. In addition to the *Journal of Social Structure*, the journal *Social Networks* (www.elsevier.com/wps/find/journaldescription.cws_home/505596/description#description) is an excellent resource as the leading international refereed journal in social networks.

In addition to the International Sunbelt Social Network Conference, many other knowledge-management conferences, such as E-Gov's Knowledge Management in Government annual conference (www.e-gov.com), offer tutorials, workshops, and/or sessions on social networks. The *MIT Sloan Management Review* and *Harvard Business Review* frequently have articles that address social networks.

Social network analysis software like NetMiner or UCINET/Netdraw will allow you to understand SNA in a more detailed fashion. Also, you may want to register on the various websites that operate on the principles of social networks, like Facebook.com, LinkedIn.com, or myspace.com. This will then allow you to see social networks in action.

Lastly, short courses and formal education on SNA are provided by various organizations, including Johns Hopkins University, the University of Virginia, IBM, orgnet.com, and many sociology programs, as shown on the INSNA website. Of course, once you become more knowledgeable in SNA, you may want to team up with those who have been conducting knowledge audits using SNA. This will build up your proficiency and confidence, and then you will climb the learning curve as you perform this kind of work on your own.

5

USING SOCIAL NETWORK ANALYSIS
IN ORG: A CASE STUDY

In this chapter we present a real case study of the application of SNA. In this case study, SNA was conducted in a major division of an international organization (pseudonym: ORG) with multiple departments and branches. The focus of the SNA was to provide a better understanding of the communication and collaboration flows in this major division.

EXAMINATION OF DATA

An SNA of employees' communication within this major division of ORG was performed by Jay Liebowitz and Aaron Parsons of Johns Hopkins University. Employees' advice-seeking communication within six distinct areas of knowledge was measured:

Context: knowledge of "what" applications
Expert process: knowledge of "how" networks and systems work
General: knowledge of "nonwork"-related activities
Process: knowledge of "how" the business works
Relationship: knowledge of "who" has information
Strategic: knowledge of "why" business opportunities reduce cost, and
   so on.

The employee data set was collected through a web-based survey. All data was downloaded to an Excel spreadsheet for examination and transformation for analysis. Two hundred and twenty-five employees answered survey questions. This provided the necessary information, as the respondents identified other employees from whom they sought a form of knowledge advice and gave details regarding the frequency and importance of the advice. All other survey respondents were removed, including respondents answering the survey multiple times. Cells containing all employee names were examined to identify abbreviated names, the use of initials, variations in spelling, and other issues in naming conventions to prevent errors in employee identification. The numbering of all names yielded 698 employees. Of those 698 employees, 473 were nonrespondents (i.e., their names were identified by those surveyed but they didn't complete a survey). All respondents provided coded information on their department and tenure, and all names were examined and hand coded for managerial status.

The data identified 1,621 knowledge advice connections or communications between the 698 employees. Each connection between employees was assigned a weight based on the frequency of knowledge being sought and the importance of the knowledge. Complete employee data for respondents, employee connections and connection weights, and nonrespondent employee numbers were loaded into NetMiner 2.5 for SNA across the six defined advice communication areas.

RESULTS OF SOCIAL NETWORK ANALYSIS WITHIN ORG

The results of the analysis of ORG advice communication data were used to answer the following questions regarding communication within ORG.

Is There a High Volume of Communication within the Division under Study in ORG?

This is difficult to derive with the existing data. Respondents were limited to identifying two persons as advice givers per area. All respondents may seek advice from more than two persons, resulting in higher levels of communication than those displayed in the data. Respondents were also not bounded within the respondent group and identified nonrespondents as advice givers. This provided a broadened network of advice givers but reduced the density of recorded communication by inserting actors who did not in turn report their communications. Density is a measure of the number of communication connections compared to the total possible number of connections within the network.

All knowledge areas examined yielded very low density or a low ratio of connections to possible connections. This was due to the abovementioned inclusion of nonrespondents, but was also driven by respondents who did not report seeking advice within some knowledge areas. This was reflected by the measure of "in-degree"—the number of connections directed at employees seeking advice. With 225 respondents, all having two opportunities to report connections, 450 connections were possible but in all knowledge areas the in-degree connections were much lower, signifying limited communication in each area (see table 5.1 for the various different knowledge types).

Is There Much Intradepartmental Communication?

Communication within departments was measured by examining the amount of communication in two areas: density and cohesiveness. "Density," as previously defined, is the proportion of all possible connections that are actually present in the network. The "cohesion index" is the extent to which ties are concentrated within a subgroup, rather than between subgroups.

Density and cohesion scores were low in all departments across all knowledge areas. This demonstrated relatively low levels of communication within departments based strictly on the number of communications occurring and when measuring communication within the

Table 5.1   In-Degree Connections per Type of Knowledge

Type of knowledge	In-degree connections
Context	323
Expert process	294
General	271
Process	246
Relationship	218
Strategic	264

department relative to communication with other departments. Within these low scores, there were departments that displayed notable cohesiveness in communication and relative density. Information security services generated cohesion scores of 1.889 and 1.625 for process knowledge and relationship knowledge, respectively. System management and business services scored a 1.375 for cohesiveness. These display relative robustness of communication between employees within these departments, but it should be noted that this is a comparison between internal communication and communication with other departments. All departments displayed low density, with the operations resilience program displaying the highest (with a density of 0.167 in both context and process knowledge).

Missing data in these areas may be contributing to these scores. Non-respondent advice givers did not have a departmental attribute. (They were clustered into a separate department coded 0.0.) This reduced the segment available for intradepartmental measures to those 225 respondents who provided complete departmental data.

Is There Much Interdepartmental Communication?

Interdepartmental communication was measured using the same format of blocking employees within their respective departments and then examining degree and density of communication between each department. Departmental communication, like employee communication within the knowledge areas, yielded low density of communication. The density of communication between departments in any area did not exceed 0.07 and the number of connections "in-degree" or communications received by departments from other departments seeking advice

Table 5.2.   Interdepartmental In-degree
Communications per Type of Knowledge

Knowledge area	In-degree connections
Context	55
Expert process	57
General	49
Process	52
Relationship	49
Strategic	49

did not exceed fifty-seven connections between the twenty-nine departments. (See table 5.2.)

Most strikingly, when assessing the data provided by complete attributes within the respondent group, some departments registered no communication with others across certain knowledge areas. These can be regarded as structural holes. (See table 5.3.)

What Kind of Communication Is Occurring between Departments?

Within the interdepartmental communications, distinct patterns of interactions between departments within all knowledge areas became apparent. Some departments played more central or powerful roles in communication within given knowledge areas. The departments were measured for betweenness, a measure of the extent to which an actor (department) lies between all other pairs of actors along their geodesic paths. Betweenness places the department in an optimal position in regard to the flow of information.

The departments were also measured for power centrality, a measure of their connectedness to other powerful departments. The departments most connected to other powerful departments are in optimal positions to receive and control information flow.

Brokerage Roles

The last measures of departmental communications were the brokerage roles played by some. These roles all define how a department

Table 5.3.   Interdepartmental Communications per Type of Knowledge

	Departments with no interdepartmental communications
Context	Technology lifecycle management
Expert process	Technology standards and development, technology lifecycle management, disaster recovery
General	IS risk analytics and reporting, technology lifecycle management, technology standards and development, disaster recovery
Process	Technology lifecycle management, disaster recovery, administration and office services relationship
Strategic	Disaster recovery, global payments and trade services, administration and office services

controls the flow of information. The categories present in the ORG departments were as follows:

Gatekeeper: contacts people outside of division and brings knowledge within

Representative: transfers knowledge from within division to another division

Itinerant: transfers knowledge between people within the same division but not within the broker's division

Liaison: transfers knowledge between people, none of whom belong to the same division

Is the Organization Well Connected among Employees?   Most communication is occurring between nonmanagerial employees. Of the 1,621 knowledge connections, 1,199 were connections to nonmanagement and nonexpert employees. Thus about 74 percent of reported advice communications were employee to employee.

Is the Organization Well Connected among Employees and Managers, Directors, and Executives?   There were 336 (of 1,621) knowledge connections (21 percent) to persons in management positions. Of 62 managers, directors, and executives, 32 were named as sources of knowledge advice five or more times. There was a greater communication rate from employees to persons in management positions than from employees to designated experts.

Are Junior Employees Interacting with Senior Employees?   Junior employees have limited contact with senior employees (executives). Employee contact is greater with other employees.

Are Directors and Executives in the "Power" Positions Centrally Located?   Executives and directors are not present or are relatively weak in most power or central positions in knowledge advice communications. A single executive and a single director appear in central or power positions in context, general, and relationship knowledge areas. Most power or central positions are held by employees or a single expert.

Are So-Called Experts Real Experts?   Within the 1,621 knowledge connections, 86 connections were to experts (5 percent). Of 67 experts, 25 were identified as sources of knowledge advice. Of the 25 experts, 4 experts were identified as sources of knowledge advice five or more times. A single expert appeared in a central position in the context, expert process, and process knowledge areas.

Are There Correlations as to Those Employees Sought Based on the Different Types of Knowledge? No evident correlation exists between knowledge type and employee attributes in central or power positions. Two persons appear in positions of centrality in three knowledge areas. A strategic planning expert appears in the context, expert process, and process knowledge areas, and a systems management and business services employee appears in process, relationship, and strategic knowledge areas.

Are There More Isolates, Transmitters, Receivers, or Carriers in the Organization? In all knowledge areas, the greatest numbers of employees are isolates. Receivers are generally greater in number than transmitters in all knowledge areas in ORG. Carriers are the fewest in number in all knowledge areas.

What Can Be Learned about the Knowledge Owners and Sharers and the Interactions of Those in the Organization Regarding the Different Types of Knowledge? Owners of knowledge are fewer in number than those asking advice. Owners span departments, not correlated to knowledge type. Owners are mostly experienced employees, but the majority are not management. Most employees do not seek knowledge from owners. Few employees act as carriers to spread knowledge.

What Were the Organizational and Individual Constraints for Sharing Knowledge at ORG? The following organizational and individual constraints for sharing knowledge were identified by the respondents:

37 percent: lack of time/work overloads
14 percent: too many silos/consolidate into central repository
10 percent: not knowing who to ask/who has the information
6 percent: job insecurity/downsizing
6 percent: getting people to share their knowledge/culture doesn't encourage it
6 percent: search engine needs to be improved/no search engine for internal info.

21 percent: other (in order):
 business processes needed/standardization/people to follow processes
 politics
 rigid hierarchical structures
 supervisor is seated away from dept./geographic dispersion
 limited access, due to security, to access intranet from home
 more communication needed between people
 need knowledge capture tool
 constantly changing organization with unclear roles and responsibilities
 need to create a continuous learning culture
 need to capture rationale why things don't work

FOLLOW-UP RECOMMENDATIONS

Further departmental examination of the SNA results could be conducted via follow-up interviews with persons identified as in central or
power positions. Also, a task analysis of these persons' performance in
the positions could be initiated. A positive reinforcement program
might be developed to create behavioral change in other positions,
based upon benchmarks set by central or power positions.

Additional recommendations to facilitate improved communications
and collaboration in ORG are to use the following:

- Portal
- Central repository
- Google-type search engine as part of the repository/portal
- Expertise locator
- Knowledge sharing recognition in performance reviews
- Lessons learned/best practices system
- Online communities of practice
- More cross-training/cross-functional teams
- More cross-departmental staff meetings
- More informal get-togethers
- Mentoring program

The knowledge management suggestions above may help to improve
knowledge and communications flow within the organization.

Table 5.4. Betweenness, Power, and Brokerage Roles in ORG per Type of Knowledge

Knowledge area	Betweenness	Power	Brokerage role
Context	Strategic planning Capacity planning	Service delivery Operations finance	Security practice and technology (Representative) Service delivery (Itinerant) Strategic planning (Liaison)
Expert process	Service delivery	Service delivery Other (29th survey choice)	Operations finance Hardware/software (Representative) Operations risk management (Itinerant) Hardware/software Service delivery Other (Liaison)
General Process	Hardware/software Enterprise infrastructure Capital market services	Network implementation Hardware/software	Network implementation (Gatekeeper)
Relationship	Service delivery Other	Service delivery	Enterprise infrastructure (Gatekeeper) Security practice and tech. System mgt. and business services (Representative) Service delivery (Itinerant) Other (Liaison)
Strategic		Central operations Application mgt. Network design Capacity planning Service delivery Operations finance	Information security services Service delivery (Itinerant)

6

KNOWLEDGE MAPPING USING SOCIAL NETWORK ANALYSIS

An important part of developing a knowledge-management strategy is creating knowledge maps of the organization. A knowledge map can take several forms. It can represent "who knows whom," "who knows what," "who knows how," and "who knows why" types of knowledge. Knowledge mapping is performed during the knowledge-audit process. As we discussed in the previous chapters, social network analysis can be an excellent technique for determining the knowledge maps in an organization.

By looking at the LinkedIn website (www.linkedin.com), one can see the value of and rapid growth of networks. Figure 6.1 shows a screen shot of my account on LinkedIn. It shows I have a few connections. However, through friends of friends, that network quickly grows to many persons. And, if I were to look at three degrees away (that is, reaching people through a friend and one of their friends), my network

Figure 6.1. Screen Shot of LinkedIn Website

expands incredibly. This is the miracle behind networking: you can rapidly expand your network.

LINKING KNOWLEDGE MAPPING TO INNOVATION

Innovation can be fostered by interactions with others. Through group dynamics, brainstorming and other creativity-enhancing techniques can stimulate new ideas and discussions. When individuals bounce ideas off each other, new products and services might come to light. Knowing who to seek out can also facilitate idea creation by allowing an individual to connect to the right people. This is where knowledge mapping can be useful.

The links between SNA and knowledge mapping have been discussed in Liebowitz (2005). Social network analysis allows an organization's knowledge flows to be mapped, which could lead to improved communication and collaboration within the organization. The IBM Institute for Business Value has been actively conducting SNA for their many clients, developing their knowledge maps and providing recommendations for improving collaboration and communication in the client organization. Under Tom Davenport and Larry Prusak's leadership, Babson College's Working Knowledge Research Center in Wellesley, Massachusetts, has been running workshops addressing SNA and strategy. At the Networks Roundtable at the University of Virginia in Charlottesville, Virginia, under Rob Cross's stewardship, SNA is the key topic as applied to innovation and strategy. Rob Cross, along with Jane Linder (research director, Accenture Institute for High Performance Business), applied social network analysis in fifteen organizations to assess how energizing interactions play a key role in creativity and innovation in organizations. Tom Davenport's work at Babson College shows how network-oriented interventions can create more high-performing knowledge workers. At Monsanto Corporation in St. Louis, Missouri, three different types of maps were created (not necessarily using SNA): "a learning map that identifies questions to be answered and decisions made, an information map that specifies the kind of information that users need, and a knowledge map that explains what users do with specific information" (www.ktic.com/topic6/13_LEAD.HTM). This latter map (i.e., the knowledge map) was used to convert information to knowledge (that is, it mapped actionable information).

Through SNA and knowledge mapping, various patterns can be identified, even a pattern such as whom individuals select as work partners. In Casciaro and Lobo's research (2005), they found that work partners are selected not so much for ability but for likability. Their study of ten thousand work relationships in five organizations shows that the lovable fool is preferred over the competent jerk. Casciaro and Lobo determined that through coaching—and while taking "likability" into consideration as critical in establishing relationships—social networks can be formed that facilitate the proper functioning of an organization.

According to Uzzi and Dunlap (2005), networks deliver three unique advantages to an individual: private information, access to diverse skill sets, and power. Strong personal networks have to be carefully constructed. Research shows that if you create your networks with trust, diversity, and brokerage, you can raise your level of information from what you know to whom you know (Uzzi and Dunlap, 2005). Hislop (2005) discusses the importance of network size on intranetwork knowledge processes. As network size increases, network density is likely to decrease, which suggests that the sharing of tacit and complex knowledge within the networks will likely become poorer. Nissen (2006) further echoes the importance of knowledge flows, stating that the impact of knowledge management increases in direct proportion to the reach of knowledge flows through an organization.

SOME EXAMPLES

ABC Corporation

Figures 6.2 through 6.5 show the results of an SNA charted using NetMiner. This SNA was conducted on an organization we'll call ABC Corporation (a pseudonym). These figures represent knowledge maps of various types of knowledge flows through individuals, departments, and management levels.

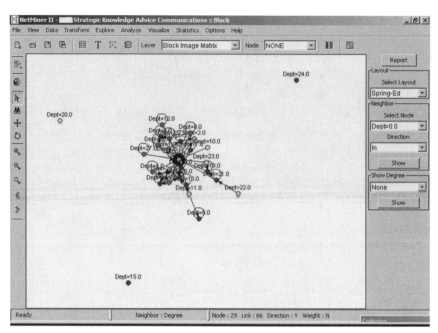

Figure 6.2. Flow of Strategic Knowledge (Centrality) among Departments at ABC Corporation

Figure 6.2 shows the flow of strategic knowledge among the various departments in ABC Corporation. In terms of centrality, there is a fair amount of clustering among the departments in terms of the sharing of strategic knowledge. However, a few departments (departments 24, 20, and 15) are outliers and could be considered structural holes as they are not part of the flow of strategic knowledge in the organization. If department 24 (or 20 or 15) were the strategic planning department, for example, this may warrant a closer look, as the strategic planning department should probably be at the hub of the strategic knowledge flow.

Figure 6.3 shows the betweenness measure of expert process knowledge flow between departments. Department 26, at the center of the web-circle diagram, is the key department in terms of betweenness centrality in this knowledge area. A few other departments, like departments 29, 14, 5, 20, 11, and 21, have relatively high scores of betweenness as compared with most of the other departments. Department 26, however, seems to carry the highest betweenness weight in terms of its relationships with other departments.

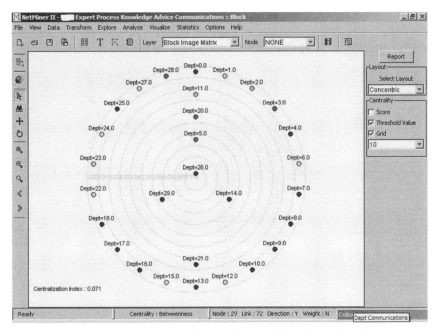

Figure 6.3. Betweenness Measure of Expert Process Knowledge Flow between Departments at ABC Corporation

Figure 6.4 is another look at ABC Corporation. This figure charts the sharing of process knowledge between junior and senior employees. The three-dimensional figure shows the junior employees (in terms of their tenure in the organization) in the larger cube; each ball represents an employee. The smaller cube shows the senior employees who have a sharing relationship with the junior employees in terms of process knowledge. Curiously, when we look at the flow of strategic knowledge between "junior" and "senior" employees in the organization, there is relatively little communication between them. Only four senior employees have this type of relationship with some junior employees. One would hope that there would be more ties between the junior and senior employees. Actually, when looking at other types of knowledge (i.e., context, relationship, expert, etc.), there are also very few connections between the senior and junior employees at ABC Corporation. In fact, the SNA showed that the main type of knowledge passed from the managers, directors, and executives to the junior employees was process knowledge. This is more tactical, administrative knowledge, versus the strategic

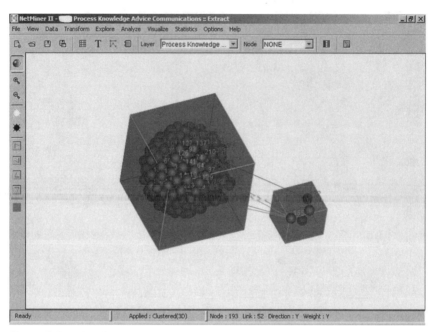

Figure 6.4. Junior–Senior Employee Sharing of Process Knowledge at ABC Corporation

knowledge that senior management should impart on the junior employees. Perhaps a formal mentoring program, cross-functional teams, or cross-departmental staff meetings would allow greater social networking and knowledge sharing to take place.

The last figure derived from the SNA of the ABC Corporation, figure 6.5, shows the flow of context knowledge between employees in various departments and levels of the corporation. Figure 6.5 shows that employee number 158 has the highest in-degree centrality compared with the other employees.

British Aerospace

J. Gordon (2000) defines a knowledge map as relying on the principle of learning dependency or prerequisite knowledge. Gordon discusses a knowledge mapping project at British Aerospace that was conducted to determine the amount of expert-level knowledge that was being shared with other organizations and its value. Based on in-

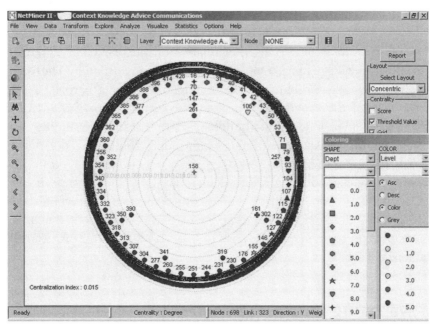

Figure 6.5. Flow of Context Knowledge (Centrality) between Employees in Various Departments and Levels in ABC Corporation

formation gathered via interviewing techniques, a knowledge map was created in which prerequisite knowledge was depicted as directional arcs between nodes. The resulting knowledge map "showed clusters of knowledge, identified high-risk knowledge, and allowed managers to discuss what part of the knowledge was essential to the company and what part was not" (J. Gordon, 2000). British Aerospace estimated the value of the knowledge contained within the knowledge map to be at least a six-figure sum.

Figure 6.6. Partial Knowledge Map Created Using Personal Brain

OTHER TOOLS FOR CREATING KNOWLEDGE MAPS

Various software tools besides SNA-related software can be used to help visualize knowledge maps. One such tool is Personal Brain by TheBrain Technologies (www.thebrain.com). Figure 6.6 shows a partial knowledge map of the functional processes used in developing a SMART knowledge-management methodology (with SMART standing for Strategize-Model-Act-Revise-Transfer). Under "strategize," the figure shows two important steps: conducting an organizational cultural assessment, and conducting a knowledge audit. In the software, if you click on these various nodes, other nodes pivot, and the diagram can zoom in or out. In general, a knowledge map can be used to highlight islands of expertise and suggest ways to build bridges to increase knowledge sharing.

DEVELOPING KNOWLEDGE MAPS

Knowledge can be located in a variety of areas: processes, relationships, policies, people, documents, conversations, customers, suppliers, competitors, and other sources. Denham Grey (2006) suggests some key questions a researcher should ask his or her subjects when performing knowledge mapping:

- What type of knowledge is needed to do your work?
- Who provides it, where do you get it, how does it arrive?
- What do you do, how do you add value, what are the critical issues?
- What happens when you are finished?
- How can the knowledge flow be improved, what is preventing you from doing more, better, faster?
- What would make your work easier?
- Who do you go to when there is a problem? (www.smithweaversmith.com/knowledg2.htm)

Grey indicates ways to collect the answers to these questions in order to build the knowledge map: conduct surveys, interviews, and focus groups; "observe the work in progress"; "obtain the network traffic logs," policy documents, organizational charts, and process documentation;

"explore the common and individual file structures"; "concentrate on formal and informal gatherings, communications and activities"; "gather from internal [and] external sources"; and "move across multiple levels (individual, team, department, organization)" (www.smithweaver-smith.com/knowledg2.htm).

Much of the early work in knowledge mapping comes from the concept or mind mapping community. Concept mapping was developed in the 1960s and is a technique for representing knowledge in graphs to form networks of concepts. Does this sound familiar? Social network analysis is also based on link analysis dealing with nodes and arcs/links. Here we can see that many of the underlying concepts of knowledge management are not new. Social network analysis, concept mapping, and knowledge mapping are all related.

SUMMARY

Social network analysis is a technique that should be used in developing knowledge maps. Through SNA, knowledge flows and gaps can be identified in order to encourage communication, collaboration, and sharing. Knowledge maps are an important outcome of the SNA process, and should be included in a knowledge audit. The eventual goal is to use these knowledge maps to improve communications flow so that innovation can be fostered and nurtured.

7

APPLYING SOCIAL
NETWORKING IN ORGANIZATIONS

As we've been discussing, social networking can help create a culture for innovation. In her article "The Office Chart That Really Counts" (2006), Jena McGregor cites several examples of how mapping informal relationships has sparked innovation in organizations. Solvay, a pharmaceutical and chemical company in Belgium, is using maps based on social and organizational network analysis to increase its innovation efforts and for succession planning. According to McGregor, IBM uses SNA as a management tool; through SNA, managers can survey the informal interactions between various groups of employees to promote the creation of new ideas. Kate Ehrlich at IBM indicates that companies can streamline innovation and collaboration through SNA (Ehrlich, 2006). Ehrlich elaborates to indicate that innovation has three phases: generating ideas, connecting those people with others in the organization who are translators, and delivering those new ideas. For innovation to take place, you usually want people to be more connected to those outside the group. Ehrlich indicates that maps of innovative organizations generally show more external focus than internal focus.

Rob Cross feels that "energy" is an important part of the innovation process, whereby new ideas are not only generated by, but also come to life through the energy of the innovators. Cross, Linder, and Parker

(2005) applied network analysis in fifteen organizations and found that energizing interactions affect innovation. Mak Tsvetovat and Kathleen Carley, both from Carnegie Mellon University, researched how changes in the social network could affect changes in the distribution of information and the resultant influence of knowledge disruption strategies on organizational performance, particularly in antiterrorist activity (Tsvetovat and Carley, 2005). Thomas Valente, from Johns Hopkins University, developed a social network threshold model in the diffusion of innovations (Valente, 1996). Consulting firms, including Accenture and the Boston Consulting Group, have also embraced SNA to chart internal and external networks.

Knowledge creation is a key reason why organizations are interested in social networking. Knowledge creation, through knowledge capture, sharing, and application, leads to the innovation of new products and services. To be competitive, companies must provide a climate that promotes innovation. In his article "Creating a Culture for Innovation" (2006), Arthur Ellis discusses the need to be competitive and to innovate on a national scale. In the United States, the National Innovation Act of 2005 and the Protecting America's Competitive Edge Act were enacted to allow government, industry, and academe to contribute towards an environment that stimulates innovation. Organizations must be catalysts for promoting innovation. Anklam and Wolfberg (2006) explain that, at the Defense Intelligence Agency, for example, organizational network analysis was used to create a more adaptive culture. Lea et al.'s work (2006) shows that business networks were enhanced through social network–based virtual communities.

Based on Valdis Krebs' work using the InFlow SNA tool, SNA has been used in many applications, including, but not limited to the following:

- Diffusion of innovations
- Team building
- Locating expertise
- Workforce diversity
- Organization design
- Internetwork design
- Post-merger integration
- Investigative journalism

- Knowledge management
- Leadership development
- Mapping terrorist networks
- Industry ecosystem analysis
- Discovering key opinion leaders
- Network vulnerability assessment
- Community economic development
- Discovering communities of practice
- Analyzing protein interaction networks
- Mapping and measuring information flow
- Contact tracing in contagious disease outbreaks (www.orgnet.com)

Rob Cross, from the University of Virginia and director of the Network Roundtable, indicates that there are three hidden network biases that work against innovation. As discussed by Cross at the 2006 KM in Government Conference (www.e-gov.com), the three biases include fragmentation, domination, and insularity. Cross points out that fragmentation of networks at certain points can invisibly undermine efforts to innovate along desired paths. Domination of networks by various perspectives and expertise can bias the development of certain innovations. Insularity can inhibit an organization from reaching out externally to leverage its expertise. For innovation to occur, weak ties are usually needed, which indicate the ability to reach out externally beyond one's group.

Let's take a closer look at some examples where social networking and SNA have provided benefits to organizational innovation.

SOCIAL NETWORKING AT THE WORLD BANK

The World Bank, headquartered in Washington, D.C., made a public commitment by its president to become a "knowledge bank." As such, a knowledge-management program was launched which included various components as part of its strategy. A key component was the creation and use of online communities of practice, called "thematic groups" in World Bank lingo. There are around seventy-nine thematic groups supported by the bank, and these thematic groups are essentially social networks developed around common themes (Pommier, 2002). Examples of thematic groups at the World Bank are climate change, poverty and health, pollution management, urban water supply and sanitation, social analysis and policy, urban poverty, and disaster management. The thematic groups are open to all staff.

In addition to these thematic groups for facilitating and building stronger social and organizational networks, the World Bank held knowledge fairs so that the thematic groups could display their knowledge-sharing activities to the thousands of individuals who attended. The use of knowledge fairs and storytelling encouraged the knowledge-sharing process to take place to further stimulate interaction and collaboration, and hopefully create new ideas. Organizationally, the World Bank added learning and knowledge-sharing criteria as part of every employee's annual job performance review. This emphasized the importance of the need to "share what we know." Also, knowledge coordinators were created to help thematic group leaders. A knowledge internship program was created, and a centralized knowledge-management unit helped in fostering knowledge-management activities throughout the bank.

A logical question is whether these knowledge-sharing activities have produced innovative ideas. The public sector group at the World Bank manages five thematic groups: administrative and civil service reform, anticorruption, decentralization and subnational and regional, legal institutions of the market economy, and public finance. According to the World Bank's website (www.worldbank.org), product innovations have resulted partly through the interactions in these thematic groups. For example, the implementation of the public sector strategy led to the use of several new products, like governance-oriented adjustment and investment loans. Other new product and service offerings have surely been created through the collaboration and interaction of the social networks fostered by the bank and by the various knowledge-sharing activities.

SOCIAL NETWORKING AT MARS, INC.

Ever try to get scientists, engineers, and technologists to expand their own networks to reach out across the organization and beyond? Mars, Inc., set out to apply SNA in order to encourage innovation and creativity in its research and development division. Social network analysis was used in a year-long study to find out who was working with whom and how scientists were getting new ideas, according to Susannah Patton's article "Who Knows Whom, and Who Knows What?" (2005). According to Patton, the SNA project discovered a lack of good communication between the snack food division in New Jersey and the food division in Los Angeles. Lack of communication led to some duplication of efforts.

Social network analysis was so successful in this application that Mars decided to apply it at its major meeting in Las Vegas. According to Patton's description, "three hundred research scientists from . . . Mars gathered in a Las Vegas ballroom . . . wearing name tags and working the floor. . . . Their RFID-[radio frequency identification]enabled tags lit up each time they met someone they didn't know, and their eyes widened as they watched diagrams of their social networks form on giant screens at one end of the ballroom. . . . Mars promised prizes to those with the most contact or 'points'" (Patton, 2005). The goal was to encourage the scientists to network with people within and, more so, outside their organization in order to increase innovation and employee retention.

SUMMARY

This chapter points out the following:

- Social network analysis is a wonderful technique for identifying knowledge flows and knowledge gaps in organizations to help in knowledge mapping/knowledge audits.
- The grapevine effect is stronger than the formal organization-chart effect (i.e., informal networks are stronger than formal ones).
- Social network analysis helps build a basis for developing a knowledge-management and human capital strategy.

As more organizations seek ways to increase innovation and camaraderie, SNA will become more essential as a tool for improving employee productivity and creativity. Being able to reach out to groups external to one's own area will be important if new ideas are to be instilled.

8

SOCIAL NETWORK ANALYSIS FOR CROSS-GENERATIONAL KNOWLEDGE FLOWS

With the baby boomer generation approaching retirement age, organizations will increasingly need to be concerned about age diversity, workforce development, succession planning, and human capital issues. According to the May 12, 2006, *Washington Examiner*, 40 percent of federal civil servants are eligible to retire in 2010. Many of these individuals are members of the senior executive service, the top echelon of managers in the U.S. federal government. State and local governments, as well as industry and universities, are faced with similar concerns.

A key way to address this enduring human capital challenge is to examine cross-generational knowledge flows in the organization and develop ways to capitalize and leverage knowledge from the senior employees to the junior ones. Many organizations are building attrition profiles in order to not be surprised when their experienced employees retire. Companies are instituting formal phased-retirement programs that allow employees to reduce their working hours as they near retirement, so that they can spend their activities in mentoring and sharing knowledge with their replacements. Mentoring programs, knowledge-sharing forums, cross-functional teaming, cross-department staffing, and other approaches are being applied to facilitate the transfer of tacit knowledge from one individual to another within an organization.

Social network analysis is a wonderful technique that can allow managers and senior leaders to better visualize how well knowledge flows between various employees grouped by tenure in the organization. This chapter will look at how SNA can help organizations better understand their cross-generational knowledge flows.

CROSS-GENERATIONAL KNOWLEDGE FLOWS

When organizations define "diversity," they often don't think of "age" as an important part of the definition. Typically, underrepresented groups and male/female ratios are the first things that come to mind. In today's graying population, however, organizations should give age diversity critical consideration. For proper succession planning and workforce development activities, organizations should know when their employees are likely to retire. This will allow the organization to plan transitioning and leadership succession. At the least, attrition profiles determine when employees are eligible to retire; they can also predict the likelihood of retirement. This then enables an organization to identify key pockets of expertise that may be lost due to these retirements, and the organization can develop succession planning efforts to fill these slots.

How does SNA relate to attrition profiles and cross-generational knowledge flows? Social network analysis can be used to trace the flow of different types of knowledge throughout the organization, and the knowledge flows can be characterized by various attributes, including tenure in the organization. In figure 6.4 we saw how an organization could use SNA to chart the interactions between junior and senior employees. In figure 6.2, we saw how an SNA can be used to reveal structural holes in an organization, where various individuals or departments are not in the flow of various types of knowledge. Thus, an SNA can be a powerful tool to help visualize where there are knowledge gaps in an organization.

We already know that SNA has been applied in a number of ways as analysts look for connections, not just with cross-generational knowledge flows. For example, Alexander Dryer (2006) discusses how SNA is being used by the National Security Agency to look for connections be-

Table 8.1.   Layers of Knowledge from Bottom Up (Hierarchical)

Knowledge that contributes to individual development
Knowledge that contributes to team development
Knowledge that contributes to work unit development
Knowledge that contributes to organizational development
Knowledge that contributes to global conglomerate/enterprise-wide development

tween phone records and possible terrorists. Google uses "centrality measures" in its PageRank system, and Jana Diesner and Kathleen Curley at Carnegie Mellon University are using SNA on the Enron e-mail corpus (www.casos.cs.cmu.edu/projects/Enron/index.php). Certainly, SNA can be of great assistance if one wants to see how knowledge is shared, transferred, and leveraged among junior and more senior employees. For example, one might depict knowledge and various holders of knowledge as shown in tables 8.1 and 8.2.

The "who knows whom" knowledge, associated with the "networker" profile, could refer to relationship knowledge. The "who knows what" could be the subject-matter expertise knowledge. The "who knows how" may refer to process knowledge, and the "who knows why" and "who knows when" could represent strategic knowledge. Social network analysis could be used to map these various types of knowledge across the layers of knowers in the organization—namely, individuals, teams, departments, divisions, and affiliated organizations. Once this is accomplished, another slice of SNA could be applied to look at the junior-senior employee knowledge flows within the knowledge taxonomy mentioned above.

As discussed in chapter 7, Rob Cross often talks about energy as a key determinant for innovation. He has applied SNA to look at the "energy levels," if you will, that employees possess. In examining energy as a characteristic for innovation, cross-generational knowledge flows can be maximized by leveraging this energy across the organization.

Table 8.2.   Layers of Knowledge (No Implied Hierarchy)

Types of critical knowledge	Types of experts
Who knows "whom"	"Networker"
Who knows "what"	"Knowledge czar"
Who knows "how"	"Innovator"
Who knows "why"	"Philosopher-thinker"
Who knows "when"	"Intuitive feeler"

Judith Lamont (2006) mentions SNA as providing a key way to spot experts in an enterprise. Expertise exists at all levels—from the secretary or assistant who knows a particular process to get something done to someone who has forty years of experience in a specialized area. This suggests that expertise can exist at varying levels of experience and age. Cross-generational knowledge flows can therefore flow up and flow down—meaning that a junior individual in an organization may have some key expertise that more senior employees might need to possess, as well as the more senior individual imparting knowledge to more junior folks.

In addition to SNA, wikis can be excellent ways to foster collaboration among generations. Cindy Gordon states, "Overall, wikis increase the socialization process, enabling collaboration to generate at warp speed. Socialization underpins the sharing of ideas, and hence innovation capacity increases from wiki infrastructure" (2006, 26). Essentially, wikis can be used to foster innovation by allowing people to quickly generate and share ideas in a collaborative spirit, thereby crossing generational gaps through an organization.

LEARNING FROM THE MILITARY AND NASA

With many military personnel rotating every two or three years, the transfer of knowledge for proper transitioning becomes paramount. Through after-action reviews, documentation, an examination of lessons learned, and some deliberate slight overlap with those transitioning in and out, the military has been able to maintain or increase the knowledge flows and decrease the potential knowledge gaps. Other agencies, including NASA, have also adopted some of the after-action type reviews through lessons-learned symposia with project teams, as well as knowledge sharing through conversations with experienced project and program managers and up-and-coming project leaders. Sharing of successes and failures—war stories—has been effectively used in the military and NASA. The Academy of Program/Project and Engineering Leadership (APPEL) at NASA (appel.nasa.gov) has a knowledge-sharing initiative to foster the transfer of knowledge; it is especially concerned with cross-generational knowledge flows. The "graybeards" use case studies and vignettes to discuss take-away points from what they have learned to help the younger NASA generations avoid going down any wrong paths. APPEL's transfer wisdom workshops, knowledge-sharing workshops, and master's forum allow the sharing and dissemination of knowledge from more senior program/project managers to less-experienced ones. The new NASA Engineering Network (NEN) is being put in place as well to include the Lessons-Learned Information System, communities of practice, and an expertise-locator system.

Learning from others and developing a strategic human capital program are important initiatives being pursued by the government and industry. Best Manufacturing Practices (www.bmpcoe.org/) and the U.S. Department of Energy's Society for Effective Lessons Learned Sharing (www.eh.doe.gov/ll/sells/) have been around for many years. Appendix A, at the end of this book, shows parts of a Government Accountability Office (GAO) report that discusses the Securities and Exchange Commission's (SEC) approach to, and progress in, developing a human capital strategy. In developing such a strategy, the SEC's goal was to bridge knowledge and skill gaps, capture and share institutional knowledge, and apply lessons learned across workers.

Other programs that are being applied in industry or government to improve the cross-generational knowledge flows between senior and junior employees include the following:

- Phased retirement: retirement-age employees continue in their old jobs but with scaled-down hours, typically twenty to twenty-nine hours per week
- Retiree job bank: allows retired employees to work up to a certain number of hours each year without adversely affecting their pensions
- Emeritus program: as a federal retiree, the individual still keeps an office and e-mail address at his or her organization so he or she can come in periodically
- Part-time retired annuitant/project team consultant: an individual acts as part of a project team on a limited basis to share his or her expertise with the team in solving a specific problem
- Mentoring program: the individual serves as a mentor in a formal mentoring program in his or her organization

- Knowledge-sharing forums: an experienced individual would meet with a small group, once a month, of up-and-coming individuals to share stories, lessons learned, and insights
- Rehearsal retirement/boomerang job: an employee retires for a few months or a year, and then bounces back to the organization with limited hours
- Job sharing: more than one person shares a job
- Facilitator of an online community of practice: an individual acts as a moderator of an online community in his or her area of expertise
- Knowledge capture/retention program: the individual is interviewed via video and the video nuggets would be accessible over the web in his or her organization

REVERSE ENGINEERING: TRANSFERRING EXPERTISE FROM THE JUNIOR EMPLOYEES TO THE MORE SENIOR ONES

When people think of cross-generational knowledge flows, they typically think of a one-way flow from the senior employees to the junior ones. However, there is specialized knowledge, particularly in the technology areas, that the junior and younger employees may possess but the senior employees lack. Thus, instead of thinking uni-directionally, organizations should look at both bubble-up and top-down knowledge flows between the cross-generational employees. Through professional development and training, mentoring sessions, brown bag "lunch and learn" knowledge-sharing sessions, and hot-topic tutorials presented by the junior employees to the more senior ones, some of the knowledge and skills levels of the more senior folks can be brought up to speed.

Let's take a look now in the next chapter to see what lies ahead for SNA for organizational use.

9

A GLIMPSE BEYOND
SOCIAL NETWORKING

According to a 2005 article in *Business Week* ("Get Creative," August 1, 2005), 96 percent of innovation initiatives fail. Part of the reason for this failure is that people are not educated and trained on the essential skills of being an effective innovator. Denning and Dunham (2006) discuss seven foundational practices or abilities that an individual needs to become innovative:

1. "Sensing" possibilities
2. "Envisioning" new realities
3. "Offering" new outcomes
4. "Executing" plans and tools
5. "Adopting" new practices
6. "Sustaining" integration into surroundings
7. "Leading" with care, courage, value, power, focus, destiny, and speech act fluency

This innovation skill set can ground the individual with the basic skills needed to move towards being creative and thinking outside the box.

How does social networking fit into this innovation skill set? Certainly, the "executing" practice can be enhanced through social networking.

Building teams is a major part of the executing phase, and social networking can facilitate the identification of the right skill sets and people for developing the team. Failure to build trust can doom this phase, and social networking is a way to instill a sense of belonging and trust among team members.

WHERE CAN SOCIAL NETWORK ANALYSIS DERIVE ITS BEST BENEFITS?

As the threat of terrorism increases, homeland security and defense will be major application areas for social or organizational network analysis. Trying to establish links between terrorist organizations, terrorist cells, financial transactions, arms dealers, and the like will become ever more important for domestic and international security. Already, law enforcement and intelligence agencies are applying link analysis for these types of applications (such as that provided by the Analyst's Notebook by i2 Inc./ChoicePoint). This trend will continue in the ensuing years.

Another interesting use of SNA will be in the business sector, in improving the effectiveness of merged and acquired organizations. In the years ahead, we will continue to see a proliferation of mergers and acquisitions and becoming the "fittest" in order to survive will take even greater precedence. The ability for these merged/acquired organizations to perform productively will be a key factor in determining who survives the best. Social network analysis can lend a hand here in order to evaluate how people, departments, divisions, and multinational offices are collaborating in order to increase innovation and worker productivity. Knowledge flows and knowledge gaps in organizations, especially in these times of a graying workforce, can be identified by SNA. Social network analysis will also suggest ways to restructure an organization in order to eliminate structural holes in the organization.

The sciences also present an interesting environment for applying SNA. With biotech firms trying to beat each other out in shortening the drug-development life cycle and shorten the drug-to-market phase, SNA can help identify opportunities for collaboration and growth. Social network analysis can also suggest ways that allow scientists and researchers to team better in complementary areas of expertise. These interactions would hopefully promote new collaborations and innovation.

Similar to biotech firms, the medical field is ripe for improved interactions between doctors, nurses, health care providers, lab technicians, and other medical care providers. Through studies conducted by the Institute of Medicine, we have learned that medical errors are a leading cause of death. Improving communication between various medical staff could hopefully reduce medical errors. Social networking can allow improved collaboration and communication, leading to a possible reduction of medical errors and increasing patient safety.

In addition to defense, business, science, and medicine, the education field can greatly prosper from the use of SNA. Of course, sociograms—which are related to SNA—were used early on in the education field. Social network analysis can help identify improved ways for teachers to work with students in order to achieve better learning outcomes. Additionally, linking generalists with specialists to improve a student's learning experience can also be enhanced through social networking.

Of course, there are many other fields that will use SNA for personal or organizational means. Whether it is for providing a forum to discuss certain medical problems or enlarging one's network for job recruitment, social networking will continue to play a part in people's lives. Social networking may best be used to link people with common interests, as in Facebook.com. Certainly, the years ahead will provide novel opportunities for applying SNA—as we "aspire to inspire before we expire!"

Social networking should allow the building of interpersonal and organizational trust. Without a foundation of trust, knowledge sharing is difficult. One of the basic tenets of knowledge management is "sharing knowledge is power." Before people are ready to share their knowledge (unless they are educators, perhaps), a feeling of trust and reciprocity needs to be established. Some of the research indicates that people are willing to share their knowledge if they see value in the knowledge that is being shared, they are recognized for their efforts, and they feel that mutual reciprocity will be extended (versus a one-way street). Social networking can help build a sense of belonging and community, which can then lead to trustworthiness.

WHAT LIES BEYOND SOCIAL NETWORK ANALYSIS?

Social or organizational network analysis is gaining momentum in terms of being applied in a knowledge-management context—that is, how organizations can improve their knowledge flows and collaboration in order to increase innovation, improve customer satisfaction, promote employee morale, and retain knowledge for building the corporate memory of the firm. Value network analysis creates another layer of insight to see how the various business processes are adding value through the social or organizational networking. For example, what is the value to the organization or to the customer in improving a certain business process through increasing communication by enhanced knowledge flows?

Konstantin Guericke, cofounder of LinkedIn, feels that social capital accelerates idea innovation (Guericke, 2006). LinkedIn is a company that is built on the premise of developing social networks for professional growth, whether through job referrals or professional development. According to Sam Kogan, president of GEN3 Partners, Inc., thirty thousand new consumer products were introduced in 2005 (Kogan, 2006). He feels that innovation is the key ingredient that determines whether a company can survive. In the Delphi Group's "Innovation Survey Results" (Delphi Group, 2006), the Delphi Group states that most respondents to their survey (39 percent) defined innovation as a new way of thinking about the organization (a new vision or strategy). Most of the respondents (96 percent) identified brainstorming as the primary practice used to foster innovative thinking. Certainly, social networking can be a form of brainstorming that could ultimately lead to creative thinking.

People often say it's whom you know. Certainly, through social networking, your ability to augment your network and make new acquaintances is greatly heightened. This broadening and perhaps deepening of your network can allow you to interface and exchange views to foster collaboration and innovation. In the coming years, more companies like myspace.com and LinkedIn.com will be created to allow people to make new connections. Blogs and wikis will continue to gain prominence as mechanisms for sharing knowledge. Formal online communities of practice will also increase as more people exchange their knowledge.

A key part of social networking is being able to learn from others. Building the institutional memory of an organization through the codifying of shared knowledge is vital to an organization's livelihood. Capturing and applying lessons learned and best practices will help organizations build and nurture a knowledge-sharing environment. Of course, these knowledge repositories or lessons-learned systems should be proactive, using "push" versus "pull" technologies. In this manner, employees can get timely information pushed to them, without having to stop what they are doing and surf the web.

As organizations grow their "strategic intelligence," SNA will be a necessary tool for analyzing ways of improving knowledge flows and collaboration. The future looks bright for organizations that are willing to look critically at improving their innovation process. Social networking and SNA will be catalysts for maximizing the brainpower of the organization's employees.

APPENDIX: SECURITIES AND EXCHANGE COMMISSION: SOME PROGRESS MADE ON STRATEGIC HUMAN CAPITAL MANAGEMENT

This appendix has been taken from GAO report number GAO-06-86, January 10, 2006, released on February 9, 2006. The complete study, as an exact electronic replica of the printed version in a portable document format (PDF) file, can be found at www.gao.gov.

REPORT TO THE SUBCOMMITTEE ON GOVERNMENT MANAGEMENT, FINANCE, AND ACCOUNTABILITY, COMMITTEE ON GOVERNMENT REFORM, HOUSE OF REPRESENTATIVES, JANUARY 2006, SECURITIES AND EXCHANGE COMMISSION, SOME PROGRESS MADE ON STRATEGIC HUMAN CAPITAL MANAGEMENT

GAO Highlights

Highlights of GAO-06-86, a report to the Subcommittee on Government Management, Finance, and Accountability, Committee on Government Reform, House of Representatives.

Why GAO Did This Study   Corporate failures and accounting scandals led to changes in legislation governing U.S. securities markets, which resulted in increased workload demands on the Securities and Exchange

Commission (SEC). As a result, Congress provided SEC with substantial budgetary increases to obtain more resources to help fulfill the agency's mission. GAO was asked to review SEC's strategic workforce planning efforts to efficiently and effectively utilize its resources. This report discusses (1) the progress SEC has made toward developing a strategic human capital plan and (2) whether SEC uses effective strategic workforce planning principles for acquiring, developing, and retaining staff.

What GAO Found   SEC has taken steps to implement a number of strategic human capital management initiatives, including developing its strategic human capital plan. In 2004, SEC split its Office of Administrative and Personnel Management into the Office of Administrative Services and the Office of Human Resources (OHR), allowing the agency to separate its administrative and personnel functions and hire an associate executive director to focus on assessing, developing, and implementing human capital programs. In April 2005, SEC created a more structured human capital council by expanding the role of the Executive Resources Board (ERB), now called the Human Capital Review Board (HCRB). The HCRB includes senior management from all major divisions and offices, the Chairman's office, the Executive Director, and OHR and follows a more formalized and regular process for reviewing and approving human capital decisions. According to SEC, as of November 2005, the agency was in the process of creating its first strategic human capital plan, which will be based on the Office of Personnel Management's Human Capital Assessment and Accountability Framework, but it has not set a completion date.

GAO also found that many of SEC's efforts related to workforce planning to date have been consistent with five key principles for effective strategic workforce planning; however, some of these efforts were still being developed or could be improved. Specifically,

- SEC has involved top management and a variety of stakeholders during the development of its strategic human capital plan, but only some employees will have the opportunity to provide feedback before the plan is finalized;
- SEC has been taking steps to identify needed critical skills and competencies, but it lacks a formal process for identifying existing skills among staff and linking them to SEC's strategic goals;

- SEC has been using human capital strategies to address workforce needs and skill gaps, but some of these strategies have not been in place long enough to assess results;
- SEC is developing or changing many of the administrative, educational, and other requirements to support workforce strategies, particularly pertaining to the use of human capital flexibilities; and
- SEC is developing additional human capital indicators and a more formal process by which to measure the achievement of its human capital goals. However, SEC currently does not formally evaluate the effectiveness of its human capital strategies in fulfilling SEC's strategic goals.

What GAO Recommends   GAO is not making recommendations because many of SEC's human capital initiatives, including the strategic human capital plan, are currently under development. However, GAO makes observations based on our audit work that highlight areas warranting management attention, such as conducting outreach with congressional stakeholders and the securities industry, obtaining employee feedback on human capital strategies before they are implemented, and taking steps to document existing skills among staff. SEC agreed with these findings and observations.

January 10, 2006

The Honorable Todd Russell Platts
Chairman
The Honorable Edolphus Towns
Ranking Minority Member
Subcommittee on Government Management, Finance, and Accountability
Committee on Government Reform
House of Representatives

Over the past several years, in the wake of corporate failures and accounting scandals, changes in legislation governing U.S. securities markets have resulted in increased demands on the Securities and Exchange Commission's (SEC) regulatory capacity. Through the Sarbanes-Oxley Act of 2002 (Sarbanes-Oxley), Congress augmented SEC's responsibilities but also authorized a substantial budget increase for the agency to better address workload challenges. In fiscal year 2003, SEC received $716 million, or a 39 percent increase over its previous year's budget authority, and has used much of it to fund more than 842 new staff positions. In addition, SEC used a portion of the fiscal year 2003 appropriations to fund its new pay parity authority, which allowed the agency to pay staff commensurate with other federal financial regulators. In fiscal year 2004, SEC received a 13 percent increase over its previous year's budget authority. These increases offered SEC a unique opportunity to obtain the resources and expertise necessary to meet its mission, but the transformation will require a rigorous effort to recruit, hire, and retain the right staff with the right expertise to fulfill agency mission and strategic goals.

In formalizing its strategic direction, on July 9, 2004, SEC approved its 2004–2009 strategic plan, which identifies the vision, mission, values, and goals shaping the agency's activities during the next 5 years. The fourth goal of the strategic plan outlines SEC's commitment to maximize the use of SEC resources. It further states that in an effort to attract, hire, and retain the right staff with the expertise necessary to carry out its mission, the agency plans to use a variety of human capital strategies that will complement the agency's other ongoing activities. To respond to your request to review SEC's strategic workforce planning, our report discusses the following: (1) the progress SEC has made toward developing a strategic human capital plan and (2) whether SEC uses effective strategic workforce planning practices for acquiring, developing, and retaining staff.

To address the first objective, we collected information and data from representatives of SEC's Offices of the Chairman and Executive Director, SEC's Office of Human Resources (OHR), and key divisions and offices on the agency's recent workforce planning activities. To gain insights on SEC's progress in this area, we also reviewed SEC's strategic plan, budget requests, and other relevant documents, and GAO reports. To address the second objective, we compared SEC's workforce planning activities with five key principles for effective strategic workforce planning, which we developed based on our review of studies by leading workforce planning organizations and interviews with officials from the Office of Personnel Management (OPM) and the National Academy of Public Administration.[1] We identified related tasks for each principle (described in our prior work) to provide more specific examples of how each principle may be implemented and we determined whether SEC was undertaking these or similar tasks. In addition, we interviewed representatives from the Office of Management and Budget (OMB) and OPM to discuss SEC's activities and best practices in strategic workforce planning in the federal government. This report primarily focuses on strategic workforce planning efforts under the former Chairman, whose resignation was effective June 30, 2005. We conducted our work in Washington, D.C., from April 2005 through November 2005 in accordance with generally accepted government auditing standards.

BACKGROUND

SEC was created by Congress in 1934 primarily to protect investors; maintain fair, honest, and efficient securities markets; and facilitate capital formation. SEC's oversight responsibilities include rule making, surveilling the markets, interpreting laws and regulations, reviewing corporate filings, conducting inspections and examinations, and determining compliance with federal securities laws. In addition, SEC monitors and regulates a variety of key market participants, which as of July 2004 included more than 7,200 broker-dealers, 900 transfer agents, almost 500 municipal and government securities dealers, and self-regulatory organizations (SRO).[2] However, as we have reported previously, SEC has faced resource and management challenges that affected its ability to achieve its mission. The following sections include a discussion of SEC's organizational structure and its human capital challenges, as well as a discussion of principles for human capital management and planning.

SEC Staff and Organization

As of August 2005, SEC had approximately 3,800 staff working in four divisions and 21 offices in Washington, D.C., and 11 regional and district offices. Approximately 41 percent of staff were attorneys, 25 percent were accountants or financial analysts, and 6 percent were investigators or examiners. The remaining 28 percent were other professional, technical, administrative, and clerical staff. Figure 1 depicts SEC's organizational structure, including the Chairman's office and the agency's key divisions and offices. [See original PDF for full image of figure 1.]

The Managing Executive for Operations and Management, who works in the Office of the Chairman, is responsible for overseeing all efforts to enhance agency productivity, retain qualified staff, and manage agency resources. In coordination with the Office of the Executive Director, the Managing Executive for Operations and Management has primary responsibility for OHR, which develops, implements, and evaluates SEC's programs for human resource and personnel management.

SEC Human Capital Management and Challenges

Over the past years, we have produced several reports relevant to human capital and workforce planning issues at SEC. In 2001, we recommended that the Chairman of SEC include a strategy for succession planning and develop a comprehensive, coordinated workforce planning effort as part of the agency's annual performance plan.[3] In March 2002, we found that SEC had not reviewed its staffing and resource needs independent of the budget process and that SEC generally developed its annual budget request based on the previous year's appropriation, not on what the agency actually needed to fulfill its mission.[4] We also commented that SEC was making its staffing allocation decisions without the benefit of a strategic plan. We recommended that SEC broaden its strategic planning process to determine its regulatory priorities and the resources needed to fulfill its mission, including identifying the staff skills needed to do so.

In July 2004, we found that although SEC received more flexible pay and hiring authority, it continued to face challenges filling critical vacancies, such as for accountants.[5] Furthermore, we reported that although SEC's allocation of its newly authorized positions was generally consistent with Sarbanes-Oxley directions, these decisions were made without the benefit of an updated strategic plan that outlined the agency's priorities—a tool that could be used to help ensure that SEC was deploying its resources to maximize organizational effectiveness. Later, in November 2004, we reported the results of a GAO survey of human capital issues at SEC to benchmark employee views following the implementation of pay parity and several work-life programs.[6] We found that the significant improvement in employee satisfaction with compensation and work-life programs could be attributed to SEC's recent implementation of pay parity and an increased focus on the use of flexible work schedules and telework programs since 2001.

In May 2005, we audited SEC's financial statements for fiscal year 2004 and found that SEC's preparation of its financial statements was manually intensive and consumed significant staff resources.[7] To address the weaknesses found in the audit, SEC stated that it would increase the number of financial reporting staff. Finally, in August 2005, as a result of our review of SEC's facilities project management and related budget planning, we recommended that SEC complete the hiring of new positions in the Office of Administrative Services and the Office of Financial Management.

Strategic Human Capital Management and Workforce Planning

Studies by several organizations, including GAO, have shown that successful organizations in both the public and private sectors use strategic management approaches to prepare their workforces to meet present and future mission requirements. For example, preparing a strategic human capital plan encourages agency managers and stakeholders to systematically consider what is to be done, how it will be done, and how to gauge progress and results. Federal agencies have used varying frameworks for developing and presenting their strategic human capital plans.[8] More recently, various agencies have begun using OPM's Human Capital Assessment and Accountability Framework (HCAAF) as the basis for preparing such plans. HCAAF, which OPM developed in conjunction with OMB and us, outlines six standards for success, key questions to consider, and suggested performance indicators for measuring progress and results. These six standards for success and related definitions are as follows:

- Strategic alignment. The organization's human capital strategy is aligned with mission, goals, and organizational objectives and integrated into its strategic plans, performance plans, and budgets.
- Workforce planning and deployment. The organization is strategically utilizing staff in order to achieve mission goals in the most efficient ways.

- Leadership and knowledge management. The organization's leaders and managers effectively manage people, ensure continuity of leadership, and sustain a learning environment that drives continuous improvement in performance.
- Results-oriented performance culture. The organization has a diverse, results-oriented, high-performance workforce, and a performance management system that effectively differentiates between high and low performance and links individual, team, or unit performance to organizational goals and desired results.
- Talent management. The organization makes progress toward closing gaps or making up deficiencies in most mission-critical skills, knowledge, and competencies.
- Accountability. The organization's human capital decisions are guided by a data-driven, results-oriented planning and accountability system.

Strategic workforce planning, an integral part of human capital management and the strategic workforce plan, involves systematic assessments of current and future human capital needs and the development of long-term strategies to fill the gaps between an agency's current and future workforce requirements. Agency approaches to such planning can vary with each agency's particular needs and mission; however, our previous work suggests that irrespective of the context in which workforce planning is done, such a process should incorporate five key principles: (1) involve management and employees, (2) analyze workforce gaps, (3) employ workforce strategies to fill the gaps, (4) build the capabilities needed to support workforce strategies, and (5) evaluate and revise strategies. Figure 2 provides a fuller description of each of the five principles. [See the original PDF version for the complete figure.]

---

1. Involve top management, employees, and other stakeholders in developing, communicating, and implementing the strategic workforce plan.
2. Determine the critical skills and competencies that will be needed to achieve future programmatic results.
3. Develop strategies that are tailored to address gaps and human capital conditions in critical skills and competencies that need attention.

4. Build the capability needed to address administrative, educational, and other requirements important to support workforce strategies.

5. Monitor and evaluate the agency's progress toward its human capital goals and the contribution that human capital results have made toward achieving programmatic goals.

Note: In broad terms, human capital flexibilities represent the policies and practices that an agency has the authority to implement in managing its workforce to accomplish its mission and achieve its goals in areas such as recruitment, retention, compensation, incentive awards, training and development, performance management, work arrangements, and work-life policies.

Figure 2. GAO's Five Key Principles for Effective Strategic Workforce Planning

RESULTS IN BRIEF

SEC has made progress on a number of human capital initiatives and is in the process of developing a strategic human capital plan. In 2003, SEC completed a comprehensive workforce and work-flow review of the agency, subsequent to which it split its Office of Administrative and Personnel Management into the Office of Administrative Services and OHR. This change allowed SEC to separate and thereby increase its attention to its administrative and personnel functions, as well as hire an associate executive director of OHR to focus on assessing, developing, and implementing human resources programs. In addition, in April 2005, SEC created a more structured human capital council by expanding the role of the Executive Resources Board (ERB), now called the Human Capital Review Board (HCRB). In contrast to the ERB, the HCRB follows a more formalized and regular process for reviewing and approving all human capital decisions. Senior management from SEC's major divisions and offices, the Chairman's office, the Executive Director, and OHR compose the HCRB and regularly meet to discuss staffing allocations and alignment of their human capital resources and strategies to achieve strategic planning goals. Finally, as of November 2005, SEC was in the process of creating its first strategic human capital plan, which according to OHR officials, will be based on OPM's HCAAF. However, SEC has not set a completion date.

Overall, many of SEC's efforts related to workforce planning have been consistent with our five key principles for effective strategic workforce planning; however, some of these efforts were still being developed or could be improved. We found the following:

- SEC has been making a concerted effort to include various stakeholders in the strategic workforce planning process, as noted in our first principle. For instance, OHR has been working with some internal and external stakeholders as it develops its strategic human capital plan. However, SEC may also benefit from conducting outreach with congressional stakeholders and the securities industry. In addition, not all SEC employees will be given the opportunity to provide feedback during the development of the plan, but may be more involved in related initiatives. Additional employee input, which SEC plans to obtain in the future, could provide SEC with more information to determine whether workforce planning efforts are understood and supported by staff.
- Although SEC has been taking steps to identify needed critical skills and competencies, as outlined in our second principle, SEC could benefit from a formal process for identifying existing skills among staff and linking them to SEC's strategic goals. Specifically, although managers can determine knowledge and abilities possessed or needed within their divisions, SEC has not systematically collected and maintained information on employees' current skills and competencies across the agency. As a result, SEC may incorrectly estimate workforce needs and skill gaps, information that helps agencies determine appropriate human capital strategies.
- As related in our third principle, SEC has been developing and using human capital strategies to address workforce needs and skill gaps, but some of these strategies have not been in place long enough to assess results. For example, SEC recognized that the agency would benefit from the knowledge and skills possessed by individuals with business degrees. Therefore, in addition to a Summer Honors Business Program that was implemented in 2001 to at-

tract future master of business administration (MBA) graduates, OHR in September 2005 implemented a 2-year program where MBA graduates rotate through various SEC divisions as associates before being permanently placed in a division. However, it is too soon to assess the overall effectiveness of the 2-year MBA program.

- SEC is developing or changing many of the administrative, educational, and other requirements to support workforce strategies that are discussed in our fourth principle. In particular, SEC has provided some training on human capital flexibilities, considered potential improvements to the administration of these programs, and has procedures in place to promote transparency and accountability in its administration of these programs.

- SEC is developing additional human capital measures and a more formal process by which to link the achievement of its human capital and strategic goals, the importance of which are underscored in our fifth principle. Currently, SEC informally links its human capital and strategic goals during HCRB meetings. A formal linkage could help SEC to better evaluate how effectively human capital strategies are fulfilling strategic goals.

This report includes no recommendations because many of SEC's human capital initiatives, including the strategic human capital plan, are currently under development. However, we made observations based on our audit work that highlight areas warranting management attention or possible enhancements in SEC's current strategic workforce planning efforts. In commenting on a draft of this report, SEC agreed with our findings and stated that the areas of concern cited in our report would be addressed once SEC's strategic human capital planning process is fully implemented.

SEC HAS MADE PROGRESS ON STRATEGIC HUMAN CAPITAL INITIATIVES AND IS DEVELOPING A STRATEGIC HUMAN CAPITAL PLAN

SEC has shown progress on a number of strategic human capital management initiatives that could help strengthen SEC's efforts in workforce planning and is developing its strategic human capital plan. These initiatives include splitting its Office of Administrative and Personnel Management into the Office of Administrative Services and OHR in order to improve efficiency and effectiveness in both and creating a more structured and institutionalized human capital council by expanding the role of the ERB, now called the HCRB. Furthermore, SEC is in the process of creating its first strategic human capital plan. According to SEC, this plan is to be based on OPM's HCAAF.

SEC Has Developed a More Formalized Process for Strategic Human Capital Management

In 2003, after the passage of Sarbanes-Oxley, SEC undertook an extensive workforce and work-flow review, and the ERB became the vehicle through which SEC leadership met to align its programmatic goals and new responsibilities with its human capital approaches and existing and new resources. The ERB—composed of senior division managers, the Managing Executive for Operations, and the head of OHR (after the creation of that office)—met monthly and on an ad hoc basis to deal with special issues, and produced recommendations for the Chairman's approval. The 2003 workforce and work-flow review process required division and office directors to present justifications for resource requests to the ERB for the board's approval. One outcome of the 2003 review was the decision to split SEC's Office of Administrative and Personnel Management into two offices—the Office of Administrative Services and OHR. According to OHR, the separation of the office's administrative and personnel functions was made to improve efficiency and effectiveness in these functions, which was necessitated by the agency's growth of approximately 1,000 individuals after the implementation of Sarbanes-Oxley. In addition, the split created an opportunity for SEC to hire an Associate Executive Director for OHR, who is tasked with assessing, developing, and implementing human resources programs.

Following the creation of OHR, SEC broadened the role of the ERB—renamed the HCRB in April 2005—to include a senior executive review of all human capital issues. SEC staff said that the HCRB has a standing 2- to 3-hour biweekly meeting and is composed of (1) directors from the major divisions and offices—Divisions of Corporation Finance;

Investment Management; Market Regulation; Enforcement; and the Office of Compliance, Inspections, and Examinations (OCIE); (2) a designee representing the interests of the field offices; (3) the Executive Director (who serves as Chair); (4) a representative from the Chairman's office; and (5) the Associate Executive Director of OHR. According to SEC, although smaller offices do not regularly participate in the HCRB, the Executive Director is responsible for representing the interests of these offices. In addition, these offices make presentations to the HCRB on an as-needed basis.

The HCRB approves all human capital decisions, including staffing allocations. Specifically, staffing allocations and current structures for each division and office can now only be amended with the approval of the HCRB. According to SEC officials, HCRB's staffing decisions are made on a consensus rather than formal voting basis. SEC staff also said that although the commission does not directly participate in the agency's human capital planning process, a representative from the Chairman's office attends HCRB meetings. Furthermore, while the HCRB has the ability to approve staffing requests, larger allocations of staff slots and staff reorganizations are subject to final review and approval by the Chairman.

Representatives from SEC's key divisions and offices said they felt that the migration from the ERB to the HCRB was much more than a name change. Specifically, the HCRB has a greater focus on SEC's strategic needs. Management staff from several SEC divisions attributed this change to the hiring of the new Associate Executive Director of OHR, who was formerly employed at OPM and who, they felt, is aware of what OPM and OMB expect from agencies in their strategic planning and human capital management processes. One division staff representative added that whereas they felt that the ERB met more "sporadically" and many did not feel compelled to gain board approval of staffing allocations, the HCRB now meets regularly and has more "rigor and structure."

SEC Is Developing a Strategic Human Capital Plan

SEC has been developing its human capital plan to address its strategic planning goal of maximizing the use of agency resources. Specifically,

OHR officials told us that the plan will address how SEC will implement and align its human capital strategies to achieve agency mission, goals, and outcomes. OHR officials also told us that they are in the process of developing a human capital plan based on OPM's HCAAF (previously discussed in the report), which identifies six standards for success: (1) strategic alignment, (2) workforce planning and deployment, (3) leadership and knowledge management, (4) results-oriented performance culture, (5) talent management, and (6) accountability. A major component of the human capital plan, according to OHR officials, will be a strategy map and balanced scorecard to delineate and determine whether its strategies and action plans are meeting each of HCAAF's six standards. A strategy map defines the strategic objectives and associated initiatives that support the organization's vision and mission. A balanced scorecard is a management system that provides metrics and feedback about agency actions.[9] The actual scorecard uses indicators to measure the relative success of each initiative. Following this approach, SEC plans to use some indicators suggested by HCAAF to measure the success of each of the initiatives. OHR officials told us that the balanced scorecard will also focus on OHR's internal operations and the agency human capital outcomes for which it will be accountable. In early November 2005, OHR officials provided us with a draft strategy map and possible draft objectives and indicators for how OHR is planning to achieve SEC's strategic planning goal of maximizing the efficient and effective delivery of human resource services.

OHR has hired a contractor to help implement the balanced scorecard approach and plans to involve a number of internal stakeholders in developing the human capital plan, including the Executive Director, the HCRB, and a cross section of division and office managers. According to OHR officials, the contractor will interview branch chiefs and assistant directors within OHR to discuss how to apply the balanced scorecard to SEC, and will also interview managers from the divisions, but does not plan to obtain input from employees below the supervisory level. As of November 2005, OHR officials, working with the contractor, have identified a list of human capital initiatives and indicators to measure the success of these initiatives. OHR officials said that the next step is to communicate with division staff to determine the appropriate targets for these indicators. Once the development work is complete, the Executive Director will approve a presentation of the human capital plan to the HCRB. After receiving HCRB's approval, OHR will disseminate the human capital plan throughout the agency. We discuss stakeholder involvement in developing the human capital plan and SEC's communication strategy in greater detail later in the report.

Once the strategic human capital plan is implemented, SEC officials intend to update the plan quarterly and annually. The process will begin with an evaluation of the results of the balanced scorecard measures. OHR management said that the quarterly assessments of the plan will focus on SEC's ability to implement initiatives and demonstrate results in both leading and lagging indicators. OHR officials said that the office plans to conduct the quarterly review and present results to the Executive Director and then to the HCRB. OHR also stated that it plans to conduct an annual review to ensure that the human capital plan remains linked to the agency's strategic plan and to correct any gaps between the plan's human capital initiatives and the ability to meet the agency's strategic goals. In addition to data used in the quarterly reviews, annual reviews are to include input from the HCRB and use performance management data and employee focus groups to determine gaps.

Although the anticipated human capital plan should allow SEC to more consistently plan for its staffing needs and adjust staffing or program priorities, it does not appear to formally link resource needs to the budgeting process. As we have previously reported, the absence of this linkage results in reactive rather than proactive activities and planning that tends to be tactical rather than strategic. According to OHR, divisions and offices are not currently required to provide OHR with annual resource allocation information such as number of planned promotions because SEC's divisions and offices do not have staff with the expertise to do strategic human capital planning. Although OHR can provide some minimal assistance to the divisions on long-term workforce planning and linking these efforts to the budget, OHR recognizes the benefit to increasing such assistance and plans to improve its capacity to provide this guidance.

COMPONENTS OF SEC WORKFORCE PLANNING EFFORTS ARE CONSISTENT WITH ESTABLISHED PRINCIPLES, BUT SOME EFFORTS COULD BE IMPROVED

We found that many of SEC's efforts related to workforce planning were consistent with our five key principles for effective strategic workforce planning; however, some of these efforts are still being developed or could be improved. Figure 3 summarizes how SEC had incorporated GAO's key principles into its strategic workforce planning. [See original PDF for full image of figure 3.]

Principle 1: SEC Has Engaged Top Management and Expanded the Role of Certain External Stakeholders

In surveying SEC activities related to our first workforce planning principle, we found that the creation of the HCRB expanded the role of top management in strategic workforce decision making at SEC. As previously discussed, HCRB meetings create a forum for regular dialogue between OHR, key executives, and division leaders, and the HCRB now reviews and approves all human capital decisions. Moreover, during the ongoing development of its strategic human capital plan and other strategies, OHR officials said that it has also sought the assistance and guidance of various external stakeholders. In particular, SEC staff have been meeting regularly with OPM and using several of OPM's key tools to assist the development of its strategic human capital plan. According to OHR officials, they have researched best practices in government, academia, and the private sector. However, SEC may have missed opportunities to conduct outreach with congressional stakeholders and the securities industry. In addition, SEC has not fully sought employee feedback during the development of human capital initiatives and, specifically, during the development of the strategic human capital plan.

SEC Has a Formalized Process for Its Top Leadership and Executives to Establish and Implement Human Capital Strategies
In our prior work, we have found that top management clearly and personally involved in workforce planning can provide the organizational vision that is important in times of change and generate cooperation within the agency to ensure that planning strategies are thoroughly im-

plemented and sustained. Specifically, we have found that a key action in integrating human capital approaches with strategies for achieving programmatic results is the establishment of an entity, such as a human capital council, that is held accountable for linking human capital management and obtaining strategic goals.[10] As demonstrated by their new responsibilities and participation in the HCRB, SEC's key executives and top management have been actively engaged in SEC's workforce planning efforts. As discussed previously, biweekly HCRB meetings are chaired by the Executive Director. This gathering of top leadership and executives helps determine and respond to current and changing workforce needs at SEC. For example, division managers we interviewed said that during HCRB meetings, senior managers representing SEC's major divisions and offices make consensus-based determinations of staffing decisions at the agency.

In addition, the HCRB is to have a role in the development of the strategic human capital plan. For example, OHR officials said it has presented status reports to the HCRB on the development of the human capital plan. According to OHR officials, once the plan's proposed indicators and related targets are developed, some HCRB representatives will review and approve them for inclusion in the plan. Although a completion date for the plan has not been established, OHR officials said that HCRB will continue to work with OHR to make revisions and approve the strategic human capital plan.

SEC Has Been Seeking Guidance from Certain External Stakeholders and Resources In prior work, we found that agencies should engage various stakeholders to identify ways to streamline processes, improve human capital strategies, and help the agency recognize and deal with the potential impact that the organization's culture can have on the implementation of such improvements. Further, involvement of key congressional and other stakeholders during the strategic planning process also helps ensure that workforce planning efforts are clearly linked to the agency's mission and long-term goals.

In developing its strategic human capital plan, SEC has been using various methods to obtain the assistance and viewpoints of external resources. According to OHR officials, staff researched and identified a number of best practice studies from government, academia, and the private sector. For instance, OHR said that it is working with a private human capital consulting company to obtain information on best practices for integrating human capital functions at SEC. The human capital functions SEC plans to integrate are (1) selection (hiring), (2) performance management, (3) training, and (4) succession planning. These functions will be linked by a common competency platform—meaning all four functions will be linked to agencywide skills and competencies, which SEC is currently in the process of identifying. As part of the integrated human capital functions initiative, officials said SEC is planning to (1) implement the performance management system within OHR by the end of 2005 and then throughout the agency, (2) begin integrating performance management with its hiring or "selection" system in May 2006, (3) offer training that develops employee competencies used for selection and performance management, and (4) use performance management, selection, and training to help institute succession planning. OHR plans to completely implement these integrated functions by May 2007.

SEC also plans to use written guidance developed by other government agencies, including OMB, OPM, and us. Specifically, OHR plans to incorporate measures outlined in HCAAF—and developed by OPM in conjunction with OMB and us—into the balanced scorecard being developed for SEC. OHR officials said that the office has consulted with OPM staff and hired a specialist from OPM to help implement its new human capital strategies, including the development of SEC University—one of the agency's new initiatives that focuses on staff training. Furthermore, according to OHR officials, SEC formally and informally communicates with other financial regulators through networking events like the Small Agency Council, and also regularly receives operational information and survey data from other regulators, including compensation and benefit comparisons, labor relations discussions, and recruiting strategies.[11]

Although SEC has collected useful information and perspectives from various external parties, SEC has not met with congressional and industry stakeholders during the development of its strategic human capital plan. OHR officials said that SEC had not met with congressional staff to obtain their input on human capital planning at SEC and did not indicate any plans to do so since SEC has communicated human capital issues to Congress through congressional hearings and during

the budget process. In addition, OHR officials told us they have collected best practice data from the private sector through a consulting
firm, but they did not state that SEC has had discussion with industry
stakeholders on how the evolving securities market may affect SEC's resource needs.

***SEC Has Communicated Its Strategic Workforce Initiatives
Agencywide but Has Not Fully Sought Feedback from Employees
during the Development of New Human Capital Initiatives***   We
have found that an effective communication strategy will create shared
expectations, promote transparency, and report progress. In general,
communication about the goals, approach, and results of strategic workforce planning is most effective when done early and clearly. Effective
strategies also allow for a variety of two-way communication and are not
limited to top-down dissemination. Efforts that address key organizational issues, like strategic workforce planning, are most likely to suc-
ceed if, at their outset, agencies' top program and human capital leaders
set the overall direction, pace, tone, and goals of the effort, and involve
employees and other stakeholders in establishing a communication
strategy that creates shared expectations for the outcome of the process.

SEC communicates relevant information on human capital issues to
its employees not only through SEC's intranet and e-mail sent to administrative contacts within divisions and offices, but also through
other forums such as staff meetings. In some cases, issues are communicated top-down from executives to managers and supervisors, and
sometimes from managers and supervisors to nonmanagerial employees. For example, OHR officials said that the presentation of SEC's
new human capital plan is to be authorized by the Executive Director
and then approved by the HCRB. Following HCRB approval, other
top-level executives (those who are not on the HCRB), managers, and
supervisors are to participate in group meetings to discuss the plan. Finally, OHR officials said that all SEC employees are to receive electronic presentations of the plan from OHR but will not have the opportunity to provide feedback prior to the approval of the plan. In
general, informal methods of communicating human capital issues include performance discussions that occur during the employee evaluation process and impromptu communications between staff and liaisons from OHR assigned to each division.

Overall, division officials said that OHR has been sensitive about the need to communicate about human capital issues, programs, and policies. However, one division manager noted that written agency communications sometimes assume that the reader has adequate knowledge of policies and procedures. For example, while SEC provides comprehensive new employee orientation training, such training could be enhanced by providing more basic information on federal government employment. This additional training may help ensure that when there are changes or new training opportunities, employees have a better understanding of the context in which changes occur. Another division manager said that OHR should e-mail employees directly regarding training opportunities instead of delegating this responsibility to the division's OHR liaison.

Although OHR has communicated with SEC staff on some human capital matters, it has not sought feedback from all employees in the development of SEC's strategic human capital plan. Without such feedback, it is difficult to determine employees' awareness of issues and fully determine the effectiveness of such human capital approaches. As previously discussed, participation in the development of this plan will not take place below the supervisory level. Nevertheless, OHR has indicated that it plans to use some employees to help with the development of some of its integrated human capital functions, such as performance management. Furthermore, OHR officials said it plans to seek feedback from employees and to use focus groups to evaluate the success of its strategic human capital plan.

Principle 2: SEC Has Been Taking Steps to Track and Identify Critical Skills and Competencies; However, It Currently Lacks a Formal Process for Identifying and Linking These Skills to Strategic Goals

SEC has been developing tools to measure needed skills and training for its employees, but currently relies on management's informal knowledge of the skills and competencies possessed and needed within agency divisions. OHR has started interviewing division management to identify agencywide and position-specific competencies. As previously discussed, SEC also has begun to integrate its human capital functions with agencywide skills and competencies. Despite these efforts to identify and minimize gaps in workforce skills, SEC currently lacks a formal process to link critical skills and competencies to the goals and objectives outlined in its strategic plan. As a result, SEC may incorrectly estimate workforce gaps, information that helps agencies determine appropriate human capital strategies.

SEC Has Made Efforts to Identify Staff Deficiencies but Does Not Maintain Information on Skills Possessed by Its Employees
Our prior work suggests that maintaining information on the critical skills and competencies that an organization's staff possess is especially important as the environment in which federal agencies operate changes. Shifts in priorities, advances in technology, budget constraints, and other factors all affect what sort of staff agencies will need to fulfill their missions. For SEC, such information is particularly useful for determining and addressing gaps in critical workforce skills or staff and making efficient resource allocations, because SEC must respond to changing regulatory conditions requiring its attention. For example, after the Energy Policy Act of 2005 (P.L. 109-58) repealed the Public Utility Holding Company Act of 1935 (PUHCA), the statute under which SEC is responsible for regulating public utility holding companies, SEC had to assess the skills of the 24 employees assigned to work in the Office of Public Utility Regulation (OPUR) to determine where they might be reassigned.[12]

Although SEC managers indicated that they were aware of the current knowledge, skills, and abilities of staff in their divisions, OHR officials stated that the agency does not currently maintain any formal inventory of the staff's skills and competencies. Documentation of staff experience and skills may help management and OHR more effectively identify hiring strategies and training and developmental opportunities for current staff that would help eliminate skills gaps. In the OPUR case, OHR officials said it has been somewhat difficult to identify the skills of employees in this office. Nevertheless, during our interviews with divisions, senior staff indicated that, in general, they have informal knowledge, mainly through experience, of the skills and competencies of supervised staff. Also, division management said that it draws upon staff knowledge when hiring; in particular, this occurs when divisions work with OHR to write position descriptions.

Despite lacking documentation of current skills, SEC has made efforts to identify deficiencies in staff skills. For example, OHR officials indicated that its office has interviewed directors and deputy directors at the agency to identify where knowledge and skills could be improved at the agency. The interviewees identified areas needing improvement, and branch chiefs ranked them in order of importance: (1) research and analysis; (2) knowledge of SEC process, rules, and regulations; (3) decision making; (4) writing; (5) oral communication; (6) information technology knowledge and skills; (7) management/supervisory skills; and (8) institutional knowledge. In another instance, in July 2004, OCIE completed a survey of examiners with higher degrees (e.g., MBA) to determine what skills were possessed and needed in the office. Further, division staff said they contact OHR when they need to identify persons with special skills and abilities. Division staff explained that OHR helps locate staff to complete work requiring special resources. Division staff interviewed generally agreed that these liaisons have proved to be an adequate resource for locating specialized skills and abilities on an as-needed basis.

Although SEC currently does not document and centrally compile skills possessed by employees, OHR plans to use the skills and competencies needed for SEC positions as the basis for integrating the four human capital functions of selection (hiring), performance management, training, and succession planning. Furthermore, SEC plans to identify competencies that will be needed agencywide as well as for specific occupations. With the aid of a private contractor, OHR plans to conduct a competency-based job analysis for each occupation at SEC. OHR expects that, in consultation with its contractor, it will determine two or three competencies that may be applied agencywide, while other technical competencies will pertain to specific positions at the agency. According to OHR officials, the core competencies will be linked to broader agencywide strategic goals, and job-specific competencies may be linked to programmatic goals listed in the strategic plan. Eventually, all SEC employees will be evaluated through a competency-based performance management system. As part of its wider strategic human capital planning efforts, OHR is in the process of linking all of its human capital functions. These functions will be linked to the critical skills and competencies identified by the agency and provide information that can be used in all personnel-related functions. For instance, skills gaps identified by the performance management system may be remedied by hiring or training initiatives.

SEC Is Taking Steps to Determine What Critical Skills and Competencies It Needs but Has Not Linked Them to Strategic Goals   In our prior agencywide work, we have found that the scope of agencies' efforts to identify the skills and competencies needed for their future workforces varies considerably, depending on the environment and responsibilities of a particular agency. The most important consideration is that the skills and competencies identified are clearly linked to the agency's mission and long-term goals, as developed with stakeholders during the strategic planning process.

SEC has already taken some steps to identify the type of knowledge and skills that would be beneficial. As discussed previously, OHR interviewed division directors and deputy directors to identify areas where staff knowledge and skills could be improved. According to OHR officials, these interviews also led to the conclusion that management should (1) create a career development plan, (2) develop an individualized training curriculum, (3) mitigate or prevent loss of institutional knowledge, and (4) promote knowledge transfer among its employees to strategically address its future workforce needs. In addition, SEC has been conducting the triennial needs assessment required by OPM. SEC has completed the first two phases of the assessment, which gathered information from executives and supervisors at the agency. According to officials, the assessment results will form the basis for questions to ask subject matter experts. Following interviews with subject matter experts, SEC anticipates that it will distribute a survey to all employees asking them to identify the skills needed to perform their jobs. The results of this assessment are to be used by OHR to determine if SEC's existing training programs should be refocused and to identify additional courses or programs that should be developed.

Although SEC has completed its 2004–2009 strategic plan, OHR officials stated that goals and objectives outlined in the plan have not been linked to specific skills or competencies. While the strategic plan lists potential performance indicators, they are not directly linked to particular critical skills or competencies. As it develops its integrated human capital functions and determines workforce gaps, SEC plans to link the critical skills and competencies it identifies to the strategic plan. According to OHR officials, this linkage will occur eventually as competencies are determined.

SEC Is Making Efforts to Reshape Its Workforce to Increase Its Efficiency and Effectiveness through Re-engineering Work Processes   When estimating the number of employees needed with specific skills and competencies, we found, based on prior work, it is also important to consider opportunities for reshaping the workforce by re-engineering current work processes or sharing work among offices and divisions within an agency. This is particularly important to SEC as it responds to changes in legislation affecting its responsibilities and substantial growth in the size of its workforce. Re-engineering processes have been particularly helpful as SEC considers more strategically how to use employees to perform a wider variety of functions at the agency, or seeks persons with differing skills to perform certain functions. According to OHR officials, the office is trying to improve employee versatility at the agency and is currently developing a "versatility index" to measure how well employees may perform a variety of tasks at the agency.

Changes in the structure and responsibilities of SEC have contributed to some changes in workforce processes. SEC executives said that in an effort to more proactively regulate the securities industry, they are taking initiatives to identify emerging risks in securities markets and are working on creating more coordination among divisions. For example, the recently created Office of Risk Assessment (ORA) works with various divisions and offices to develop methodologies to address identified risk. ORA consults with risk-assessment committees that consist of staff from various divisions. Committees currently exist for the following areas: (1) full disclosure, (2) investment management and regulation, and (3) SEC infrastructure. ORA also uses software in coordination with divisions to identify how emerging risks have affected SEC's workload and responsibilities. However, according to SEC management, ORA is not directly involved in workforce planning efforts at the agency.

Various divisions have also modified work processes to respond to changing responsibilities and workload and identified skill gaps. For example, SEC's Enforcement staff attorneys were responsible for collecting disgorgement, as well as investigating potential violations of securities law.[13] Partly in response to the new Fair Fund provision under Sarbanes-Oxley, the Division of Enforcement hired attorneys dedicated to collections, as well as case management specialists, to assist with maximizing collections and addressing competing priorities and the growing workload of the Enforcement attorneys. Enforcement also stated that it is working with technology staff to improve systems, so that collection information is tracked in one system rather than captured in multiple systems. Furthermore, the Division of Investment Management is now conducting integrated disclosure reviews and participates in cross-divisional task forces, such as the Investor Education and Soft Dollar task forces, to leverage skills across divisions.[14] In addition, as a result of using a risk-based approach to more proactively identify and address compliance risks, OCIE recently gained the approval of the HCRB to create 20 additional staff positions, to be filled by individuals with data analysis skills to collect surveillance data. SEC is also now responsible for overseeing investment firms that want to become a consolidated supervised entity (CSE).[15] Because such oversight requires a combination of specialized technical and auditing skills currently not found within the agency, OCIE recently created a new unit to oversee CSEs.

Principle 3: SEC Has Developed Some Human Capital Strategies to Address Gaps, but It Is Too Early to Assess Results

SEC is using a variety of methods to address skill gaps and improve employee benefits and work life. For example, SEC uses its student loan repayment (SLR) program and teleworking opportunities to attract and retain employees. In addition, SEC is linking its human capital functions and focusing on developing skills and competencies to use for hiring, performance management, training, and succession planning. SEC also has been developing SEC University to expand employee training opportunities and minimize critical skills gaps. Recently, OHR has used hiring and retention data, focus groups, and surveys to assess the use of many of SEC's work-life programs. However, because many of the human capital strategies have only recently been implemented, it is too soon to assess the effectiveness of these strategies.

SEC Is Building More Comprehensive Human Capital Strategies to Recruit and Retain Employees and Address Skill Gaps   In our prior work, we have found that much of the authority that allows agencies to tailor human capital strategies to their needs is already available under current laws and regulations. Therefore, in setting goals for their human capital programs and developing tailored workforce planning strategies to achieve these goals, agencies should identify and use all appropriate administrative authorities to build and maintain an effective workforce for the future.

As mentioned earlier, SEC has been developing integrated human capital functions to better recruit and retain the right staff with the right expertise to help achieve its strategic goals and objectives. SEC indicated that selection, or hiring, is a critical tool to meet its changing needs, particularly following the increase in SEC's responsibilities under Sarbanes-Oxley. SEC made several changes to its hiring process to fill accountant positions within Corporation Finance, which had been a challenging task for the agency partly due to the slowness of the hiring process and the reluctance of some candidates to relocate to Washington, D.C. First, SEC retained an executive recruiting firm to carry out some of the recruitment. Second, to expedite the hiring process, OHR introduced an automated hiring system to accelerate the review of applications by automatically disseminating information on job candidates to Corporation Finance. Third, to accommodate qualified applicants who might not want to relocate to SEC headquarters, Corporation Finance instituted a "virtual workforce" pilot where several of its employees can work from an alternate site and physically report to an SEC location on a limited basis. OHR staff indicated that the pilot phase of the program would be useful in helping managers learn how to manage offsite employees. However, it is unclear to what extent the program will be expanded, or whether it will be continued. Finally, OHR said that category rating will be introduced to the agency during 2006.[16]

In addition to exploring ways to improve the hiring processes, SEC also has tried to more strategically allocate skills and experience when creating or filling existing vacancies. For example, recognizing the need for more administrative support for its collection program, the Division of Enforcement recently filled a number of positions with paralegals and administrative personnel instead of attorneys. SEC also recognized that as an agency, it would benefit from the knowledge and skills possessed by individuals with business degrees. Therefore, as mentioned earlier, SEC developed a Summer Honors Business Program in 2001 to attract future MBA graduates to SEC. In September 2005, OHR implemented a 2-year program where MBA graduates rotate through various SEC divisions as associates before being permanently placed in a division.

To increase employee retention, SEC has increased the use of its SLR program and telework arrangements. SEC began using the SLR program in the last half of fiscal year 2003 and reported making 384 student loan repayments totaling approximately $3.3 million in fiscal year 2004. This is an increase from fiscal year 2003, in which 257 employees received payments.[17] To receive loan repayment, enrollees agree to work for an additional 3 years at SEC. According to SEC officials, few employees leave before the 3-year employment agreement terminates. SEC is also expanding the use of telework arrangements for its employees, with approximately 20 percent of its workforce now participating in the program. As of August 2005, SEC reported having 813 approved teleworking employees, an increase from March 2005, when it had 648 employees approved for telework. SEC also found that strategic use of recruitment and retention bonuses for employees with qualifications critical to SEC's mission has been an effective way to achieve its hiring goals and an efficient use of funding.

In addition, SEC has been expanding its training programs to eliminate gaps and maximize employee contributions. Training efforts at SEC previously focused on specific division and office needs, and division managers told us they have training units within their divisions. With the development of SEC University, OHR hopes to bring about a cultural change within the agency and encourage cross-divisional and agencywide training. Although OHR plans to consolidate various training programs at SEC through the university, some divisions indicated that they found in-house training on technical issues performed by division staff critical to meeting agency goals and felt such training should remain outside the main training center at SEC. To date, OHR has taken no action to discontinue training offered within divisions. In September 2005, SEC placed a new position announcement to hire a person from within SEC who would be devoted exclusively to directing

SEC University. OHR officials expect this position to be filled by the end of November 2005. As part of the current SEC University plan, OHR is assessing employee training interests and relevancy to programmatic functions, and is exploring establishing training partnerships with government, public and private entities, and five or six law and business schools. According to OHR, SEC University also plans to provide supervisory training and help the agency maintain quality leadership, which will be particularly important because 14 percent of SEC managers will be eligible to retire by the end of 2005.

In addition to developing a curriculum for SEC University, OHR is also working to automate and centralize employees' training and skills information. OHR has proposed that SEC develop a learning management system to centrally track employees' work experiences and training, as well as provide a forum to share work experiences among employees.[18] OHR has produced a project plan outlining the business needs for the learning management system, including key deliverable dates for implementation and cost estimates.

SEC Has Various Methods in Place to Measure the Success of Its Human Capital Approach, but Many of These Assessments Are Not Yet Complete   Our previous agencywide work suggests that agencies could benefit by assessing key aspects of their human capital approach to identify possible obstacles and opportunities that may occur in meeting critical workforce needs. Specifically, an agency can use HCAAF to create indicators to measure the effectiveness of human capital approaches.

According to OHR officials, the office has used various methods to assess recruitment, retention, and work-life issues at SEC, including (1) focus group research, (2) employee satisfaction surveys on human capital flexibilities, and (3) entrance and exit interviews. OHR has conducted focus groups of employees on recruitment effectiveness, as well as retention and job satisfaction. According to OHR officials, it has used the findings from its research studies and OPM's Federal Human Capital Survey in developing SEC's strategic human capital plan.[19] For example, focus group results showed that SEC employees were most concerned about being recognized for good performance and agency procedures for dealing with poor performance. Consequently, OHR determined that performance management and training needed to be enhanced. OHR also determined that SEC needed to integrate the four human capital functions of selection (hiring), performance management, training, and succession planning. Specifically, OHR plans to enhance its performance management by using individual development plans for employees that include more comprehensive and targeted training and development opportunities.

As indicated above, SEC is using results from various surveys and informal assessments to improve human capital management. However, many of its human capital strategies are new or under development, and it is too soon to gauge their effectiveness. As part of developing and implementing its human capital plan, SEC plans to use a balanced scorecard to more comprehensively assess the effectiveness of its human capital strategies and workforce planning efforts. As of November 2005, OHR has worked with a contractor to develop a list of indicators that SEC could use to measure the progress the agency has made on its human capital strategies.

Principle 4: SEC Is Addressing Administrative, Educational, and Other Requirements Important to Supporting Workforce Strategies

Overall, SEC has been addressing many of the administrative, educational, and other requirements to support human capital programs and workforce strategies, including (1) educating managers and employees on the use of flexibilities, (2) streamlining and improving administrative processes, and (3) building transparency and accountability into its human capital system. To this end, SEC requires some training for supervisors and new employees on the use of human capital flexibilities. OHR told us that it informally reviews its administrative processes and has been working to improve the administration of some human capital flexibilities. In addition, we found that SEC has promoted transparency and accountability in the use of these flexibilities.

SEC Requires Some Training for Supervisors and New Employees on Flexibilities As discussed in prior GAO work, managers and supervisors can be much more effective in using human capital strategies that involve flexibilities if they are properly trained to identify when they can be used and how they can be administered. In addition, to avoid confusion and misunderstandings, it is also important to educate employees about how the agency uses human capital flexibilities and what rights employees have under policies and procedures related to human capital.

According to OHR officials, supervisors are usually required to attend training on policies and practices related to newly implemented human capital programs. For example, SEC has focused on strengthening its telework program. In the spring of 2005, the agency hired a consultant to develop and deliver a comprehensive training program designed to better equip supervisors to manage remote workers. SEC management said that while the training was not mandatory, supervisors were strongly encouraged to participate. In addition, management from several divisions confirmed that all of their supervisors and managers had been briefed on available human capital flexibilities at SEC, especially alternative work schedules and telework.

SEC also has disseminated information on human capital programs to new and current employees. New employees receive such information at a required orientation session. OHR officials told us that current employees can receive information concerning human capital flexibilities through administrative notices, technical training, daily consultation with OHR staff, and postings of human capital information on the agency's intranet. SEC has also been finalizing an SEC employee handbook that provides information on human capital flexibilities.

SEC Has Improved Administrative Processes That Support the Use of Some Flexibilities   As suggested in our prior work, it is important that agency officials look for instances in which administrative processes can be re-engineered to more effectively administer flexibilities. OHR officials told us that while they do not conduct a formal evaluation of the effectiveness of existing administrative processes, they do solicit feedback from divisions and agencies and adjust processes to meet their needs. For example, to expedite the hiring process for a division that had a substantial number of positions to fill, SEC delegated authority to grant recruitment bonuses to the division's director, allowing the division to more quickly and readily recruit highly desirable candidates. In another example, OHR officials told us they plan to develop and implement recommendations based on SEC managers' suggestions provided in our 2005 study of SLR programs implemented by various federal agencies.[20] Specifically, we recommended that SEC build on current efforts to measure the impact of the repayment program by determining now what indicators SEC will use to track program success, what baseline SEC will use to measure resulting program changes, what data SEC needs to collect, and whether SEC could use periodic surveys to track employee attitudes about the program.

Additionally, OHR officials said that their office has surveyed managers and employees to gauge the ease of administering policies and procedures. Similarly, OHR has asked employees hired using flexibilities (such as recruitment bonuses) and employees who participate in the telework and student loan repayment programs for suggestions to improve administrative processes. According to OHR officials, OHR plans to continue to refine collection and analysis of this information as the office develops and implements the balanced scorecard.

SEC Has Processes to Promote Transparency and Accountability in the Use of Flexibilities In our prior agencywide work, we found that clear guidelines for using specific flexibilities and holding managers and supervisors accountable for their fair and effective use are essential for successfully implementing workforce strategies. SEC has some processes in place to promote transparency and accountability in the use of flexibilities. According to SEC management, key stakeholders—OHR staff, Employee-Labor Relations (ELR) specialists, managers, and senior management officials—have assisted in developing guidelines for using flexibilities. In addition, OHR officials told us that the National Treasury Employees Union, the labor organization that represents SEC employees, is involved in all matters affecting employees in the union.[21]

In using human capital flexibilities, SEC generally requires employees to prepare and submit a written request that must then receive managerial approval and, in some cases, input from ELR as well as OHR. To help ensure accountability in the use of flexibilities, employees' requests go through more than one level for approval or disapproval. For example, to telework, employees first submit a written request to their immediate supervisor, who then forwards it to a second-level supervisor for final approval or disapproval. If the request is denied, the second-level supervisor must document why. If there is a "close call" in approving or denying a telework request, ELR or OHR staff may be consulted. SEC officials told us that ELR usually gets involved when a request is denied. According to SEC officials, the agency requires written justification for denials of employee application for most types of flexibilities, not just telework.

Outside agencies also play a role in ensuring accountability in SEC's use of human capital policies, programs, and options. SEC's use of flexibilities is subject to review by OPM, OMB, the Merit Systems Protection Board, Congress, and us. Specifically, OPM monitors SEC's use of direct hire authority, as well as student loan repayment. Moreover, according to SEC, unionized employees can file a grievance under the provisions of the collective bargaining agreement, and there is an administrative grievance process in place for nonunionized employees.

Principle 5: SEC Is Developing Additional Human Capital Measures and a Formal Process by Which to Link the Achievement of Its Human Capital and Strategic Goals

Our prior agencywide work found that agencies should develop appropriate performance measures to link human capital measures with strategic goals. Performance measures, appropriately designed, can be used to gauge success and evaluate the contribution of human capital activities toward achieving programmatic goals. SEC management said that SEC has informally monitored the agency's progress toward achieving some human capital goals using a few performance measures. SEC mainly has monitored hiring, attrition, and retention rates. These indicators, along with other indicators compiled by the divisions and offices to measure performance related to programmatic goals, compose SEC's management "dashboards." The "dashboards" are indicators compiled monthly by the Executive Director's office and are designed to present regular snapshots of the divisions' and offices' progress in meeting budget, staffing, and performance objectives. One division official said that the turnover rates and measures of supervisors' tenure included in the dashboards were particularly useful. Division managers said they consulted with OHR when the human capital indicators identified potential issues. For example, a division manager we interviewed noted that one human capital measure indicated few women in the division were applying for branch chief jobs, and the division has been working with OHR to determine the reasons why.

Although SEC uses some human capital indicators, OHR officials acknowledged that they needed to develop additional measures because their current indicators capture output measures for overall human capital strategies, such as turnover, but do not directly link to specific human capital initiatives. OHR officials explained that the balanced scorecard, discussed earlier, will link human capital initiatives to outcomes. Identifying performance measures and discussing how the agency will use them to evaluate the human capital strategies—before it starts to implement the strategies—can help agency officials think through the scope, timing, and possible barriers to evaluating the workforce plan. However, as we have found in prior work, developing meaningful outcome-oriented performance measures for both human capital and programmatic goals, and collecting performance data to measure achievement of these goals are major challenges for many federal agencies.

Further, one SEC division official said it was particularly difficult to develop performance measures in areas dealing with the enforcement of laws and regulations. For example, in 2002 we reported that SEC strategic and annual performance plans did not clearly indicate the priority that disgorgement collections should receive in relation to SEC's other goals and did not include collection-related performance measures.[22] In our 2005 report, we found that SEC needed to make further progress in establishing performance measures to better track the effectiveness of its collection efforts, and track both receivers' fees and the amounts distributed to harmed investors.[23]

Finally, SEC said that evaluations of the linkage between human capital and strategic goals currently take place informally during various meetings, including HCRB meetings, and the results of these evaluations are addressed through periodic adjustments made to deal with short-term problems. More specifically, SEC management said that HCRB members used the management "dashboards" to help make staffing decisions, but noted that the dashboards were not tightly linked to the HCRB process. However, OHR anticipates that the implementation of the balanced scorecard and its indicators will strengthen and formalize the linkage between human capital activities and strategic goals.

OBSERVATIONS

With the enhancements being made to its human capital management, SEC has begun to use a planning and management approach that ensures ongoing attention to human capital issues. SEC has been making changes to ensure management focuses not only on traditional personnel functions, but also on the broader issues of human capital management. Further, senior managers are beginning to focus on strategic issues in decision making. In particular, SEC has undertaken a number of initiatives that demonstrate its commitment to human capital planning. When enacted, these initiatives should begin to help address the agency's human capital challenges, some of which are long-standing and cannot be quickly or easily overcome, such as succession planning. To ensure the success of SEC's strategic goals, it is critical that SEC complete its human capital initiatives—in particular, its strategic human capital plan. A well-documented plan is an essential tool that can serve as a guide for SEC in workforce management and direct an effective, ongoing communications strategy that genuinely engages employees and other stakeholders in the creation and administration of human capital programs.

Based on our discussions with OHR, SEC is in the process of creating a human capital plan. SEC's finalized human capital plan is to include many of the best practices outlined in our five principles for workforce planning. While we are encouraged by SEC's progress, three areas may warrant management attention as SEC continues to develop its human capital plan: conducting outreach with congressional stakeholders and the securities industry on strategic workforce planning, obtaining employee feedback on human capital strategies before they are implemented, and taking steps to better identify, understand, and document existing skills among staff. Obtaining feedback from congressional stakeholders and the securities industry could enhance SEC's ability to gain feedback from these important groups. Further, employee input prior to implementation may increase SEC's ability to determine whether its human capital strategies are understood and supported by the staff. In addition, by formally identifying and documenting existing skills among staff, SEC may more accurately estimate workforce needs and skill gaps, which is information that helps agencies determine appropriate human capital strategies. Finally, we want to stress the importance of ensuring that the plan formally links human capital activities with the goals in SEC's strategic plan. This linkage will help SEC to use its workforce to increase the agency's operational effectiveness and responsiveness.

APPENDIX I: SCOPE AND METHODOLOGY

In order to describe the progress the Securities and Exchange Commission (SEC) made in developing a strategic human capital plan, we gathered and analyzed data from a variety of sources. We reviewed GAO's recent prior work on human capital issues at SEC. We also obtained information on SEC's operations and strategic planning efforts, recent budget requests, human capital plans and strategies, workforce data, milestones and timelines, and performance measures. To collect data not identified through prior work, we contacted and conducted interviews with SEC, the Office of Management and Budget (OMB), and Office of Personnel Management (OPM) to obtain relevant information.

To evaluate how SEC was developing its long-term strategies for acquiring, developing, and retaining staff to achieve the agency's mission, we used the key principles for effective strategic workforce planning developed in *Human Capital: Key Principles for Effective Strategic Workforce Planning* as our criteria for identifying workforce planning practices that SEC planned or had under way.[24] Using these five principles, we also identified related tasks associated with each principle to provide more specific examples of how each principle might be implemented.

Additionally, we met with SEC, OPM, and OMB to discuss and collect information on the agency's former and current practices and future plans to address human capital issues. After these initial meetings, we held follow-up meetings with SEC's Office of Human Resources and other key offices and divisions to gather relevant information.

We conducted our work in Washington, D.C., from April 2005 through November 2005 in accordance with generally accepted government auditing standards.

GAO CONTACT

Orice M. Williams, (202) 512-8678 or williamso@gao.gov

STAFF ACKNOWLEDGMENTS

In addition to the contact named above, Karen Tremba, Assistant Director; Allison Abrams; Marianne Anderson; William R. Chatlos; Kenneth Scott Derrick; Marc Molino; and Barbara Roesmann made key contributions to this report.

NOTES

1. GAO, *Human Capital: Key Principles for Effective Strategic Workforce Planning*, GAO-04-39 (Washington, D.C.: Dec. 11, 2003).

2. SROs are organizations responsible for regulation of member broker-dealers. Among other things, transfer agents cancel stock certificates presented for transfer, issue new stock certificates, and maintain records reflecting the ownership of securities as agent for the issuers.

3. GAO, *Securities and Exchange Commission: Human Capital Challenges Require Management Attention*, GAO-01-947 (Washington, D.C.: Sept. 17, 2001).

4. GAO, *SEC Operations: Increased Workload Creates Challenges*, GAO-02-302 (Washington, D.C.: Mar. 5, 2002).

5. GAO, *Securities and Exchange Commission: Review of Fiscal Year 2003 and 2004 Budget Allocations*, GAO-04-818 (Washington, D.C.: July 23, 2004).

6. GAO, *Securities and Exchange Commission Human Capital Survey*, GAO-05-118R (Washington, D.C.: Nov. 10, 2004). Work-life programs help employees balance their work and family lives and include compressed work schedules, alternative work schedules, telecommuting, and part-time work arrangements.

7. GAO, *Financial Audit: Securities and Exchange Commission's Financial Statements for Fiscal Year 2004*, GAO-05-244 (Washington, D.C.: May 26, 2005).

8. For example, in a March 2002 exposure draft, we introduced a strategic human capital model designed to help agency leaders effectively use their people and determine how well they integrate human capital considerations into

daily decision making and planning for the program results they seek to achieve. This model is built around four cornerstones: (1) leadership; (2) strategic human capital planning; (3) acquiring, developing, and retaining talent; and (4) results-oriented organizational cultures.

9. A balanced scorecard provides feedback for both internal organizational processes and external outcomes in order to continuously improve strategic performance and results. Generally, the balanced scorecard approach suggests that the agency view its organization from four perspectives and develop metrics, collect data, and analyze itself relative to each perspective: (1) learning and growth, (2) business process, (3) customer perspective, and (4) financial perspective.

10. GAO, *Human Capital: Selected Agency Actions to Integrate Human Capital Approaches to Attain Mission Results*, GAO-03-446 (Washington, D.C.: Apr. 11, 2003).

11. The Small Agency Council is the voluntary management association of independent sub-Cabinet federal agencies. Established in 1986, the council represents about 80 small agencies. Members have diverse program responsibilities that include public- and private-sector employment, commerce and trade, energy and science, transportation, national defense, and finance and cultural issues. Almost half of the council's members are regulatory or enforcement agencies.

12. As a result of PUHCA being repealed, SEC will transfer responsibility for regulating these entities to the Federal Energy Regulatory Commission in February 2006.

13. Section 308(a) of Sarbanes-Oxley, the Federal Account for Investor Restitution provision, commonly known as the Fair Fund provision, allows SEC to combine civil monetary penalties and disgorgement amounts collected in enforcement cases to establish a fund for the benefit of victims of securities law violations. Disgorgement is a remedy designed to deprive defendants of their ill-gotten gains derived from their illegal activities.

14. Broker-dealers typically provide a bundle of services, including research and execution of transactions, that are paid for by broker-dealers' commissions. "Soft dollars" are commission dollars that broker-dealers allocate to pay for the research component.

15. GAO, *Financial Regulation: Industry Changes Prompt Need to Reconsider U.S. Regulatory Structure*, GAO-05-61 (Washington, D.C.: Oct. 6, 2004). Many of the largest financial legal entities are part of holding company structures—companies that hold stock in one or more subsidiaries. Holding companies that own large broker-dealers can elect to be supervised by SEC as consolidated supervised entities. SEC would provide groupwide oversight

of these entities unless they are determined to already be subject to "comprehensive, consolidated supervision" by another principal regulator.

16. Category rating allows agencies to place job candidates in broad quality groupings rather than assigning candidates actual numerical ratings. This approach may give the selecting officials more candidates from whom to select rather than limiting agency officials to just the top three, as is the case with the traditional federal hiring system.

17. GAO, *Federal Student Loan Repayment Program: OPM Could Build on Its Efforts to Help Agencies Administer the Program and Measure Results*, GAO-05-762 (Washington, D.C.: July 22, 2005).

18. According to SEC, a learning management system automates the administration of learning processes to plan, register, deliver, and measure courseware. It provides the ability to create, store, access, and reuse learning content. Such a system can provide collaboration and communication tools for participants and instructors to interact and share information from different locations, as well as provide access to information, tools, and processes on the job, where it is most used.

19. The Federal Human Capital Survey is a biennial survey of federal employees that measures employees' perceptions of whether, and to what extent, conditions characterizing successful organizations are present in their agencies.

20. GAO-05-762.

21. SEC officials estimate that two-thirds of SEC's 4,000 employees are members of the union.

22. GAO, *SEC Enforcement: More Actions Needed to Improve Oversight of Disgorgement Collections*, GAO-02-771 (Washington, D.C.: July 12, 2002).

23. GAO, *SEC and CFTC Penalties: Continued Progress Made in Collection Efforts, but Greater SEC Management Attention Is Needed*, GAO-05-670 (Washington, D.C.: Aug. 31, 2005).

24. GAO-04-39. This is a work of the U.S. government and is not subject to copyright protection in the United States. It may be reproduced and distributed in its entirety without further permission from GAO.

REFERENCES

Amidon, Debra M. 1999. "Knowledge Innovation," *Entovation International*, at www.entovation.com/innovation/knowinno.htm.

Anklam, P., and A. Wolfberg. 2006. "Creating Networks at the Defense Intelligence Agency," *KM Review* 9, no.1, March/April.

Awazu, Y. 2004. "Knowledge Management in Distributed Environments: Roles of Informal Network Players," *Proceedings of the 37th Hawaii International Conference on System Sciences.* New York: IEEE Press.

Casciaro, T., and M. S. Lobo. 2005. "Competent Jerks, Lovable Fools, and the Formation of Social Networks," *Harvard Business Review*, June.

Cross, R., and A. Parker. 2004. *The Hidden Power of Social Networks.* Cambridge, MA: Harvard Business School Press.

Cross, R., J. Linder, and A. Parker. 2005. "Charged Up: Managing the Energy that Drives Innovation," The Network Roundtable white paper, University of Virginia, Charlottesville, VA, at www.networkroundtable.org.

Delphi Group. 2006. "Innovation Survey Results," white paper, The Information Intelligence Summit, April 10–13, The Delphi Group, Phoenix, AZ.

Denning, P., and R. Dunham. 2006. "Innovation as Language Action," *Communications of the ACM* 49, no. 5, ACM Press, New York, May.

Dryer, Alexander. 2006. "How the NSA Does Social Network Analysis," *Slate,* May 15, at www.slate.com/id/2141801.

Ehrlich, Kate. 2006. "IBM: Untangling Office Connections," *BusinessWeek Online*, February 17, at www.businessweek.com.

Ellis, Arthur. 2006. "Creating a Culture for Innovation," *Chronicle of Higher Education*, April 14.

Ensign, P., and L. Hebert. 2004. "Knowledge Sharing among R&D Scientists," *Proceedings of the 37th Hawaii International Conference on System Sciences*. New York: IEEE Press.

Farnham, S., S. Kelly, W. Portnoy, and J. Schwartz. 2004. "Wallop: Designing Social Software for Co-located Social Networks," *Proceedings of the 37th Hawaii International Conference on System Sciences*. New York: IEEE Press.

Gordon, Cindy. 2006. "Wikis—a Disruptive Innovation," *KMWorld*, June.

Gordon, J. 2000. "Creating Knowledge Maps by Exploiting Dependent Relationships," *Knowledge-Based Systems Journal* 13, Elsevier.

Grey, Denham. 2006. *Knowledge-at-Work*, at denham.typepad.com.

Guericke, K. 2006. "The Link between Social Capital, Information, and Innovation," Information Intelligence Summit, April 10–13, The Delphi Group, Phoenix, AZ.

Hislop, D. 2005. "The Effect of Network Size on Intra-Network Knowledge Processes," *Knowledge Management Research & Practice Journal*, Palgrave Publishing, November.

Kelley, Tom. 2001. *The Art of Innovation*. New York: Doubleday.

Kogan, S. 2006. "Organizing and Managing Knowledge for Product Innovation," Information Intelligence Summit, April 10–13, The Delphi Group, Phoenix, AZ.

Lamont, Judith. 2006. "Finding Experts—Explicit and Implicit," *KMWorld*, June.

Lea, B. R., W. B. Yu, N. Maguluru, and M. Nichols. 2006. "Enhancing Business Networks Using Social Network Based Virtual Communities," *Industrial Management & Data Systems Journal* 106, no. 1, Emerald Group Publishing, Bradford, UK.

Liebowitz, J. 2005. "Linking Social Network Analysis with the Analytic Hierarchy Process for Knowledge Mapping in Organizations," *Journal of Knowledge Management* 9, no. 1, Emerald Intelligence, UK.

McGregor, Jena. 2006. "The Office Chart That Really Counts," *BusinessWeek Online*, February 27, at www.businessweek.com.

Naisbitt, John, and Patricia Aburdene. 1985. *Re-inventing the Corporation: Tranforming Your Job and Your Company for the New Information Society*. New York: Warner Books.

Nissen, M. 2006. *Harnessing Knowledge Dynamics*. Hershey, PA: IRM Press.

Patton, Susannah. 2005. "Who Knows Whom, and Who Knows What?" *CIO Magazine*, June 15, at www.cio.com/archive/061505/km.html.

Pommier, M. 2002. "How the World Bank Launched a Knowledge Management Program," Knowledgepoint, at www.knowledgepoint.com.au.

Tsvetovat, M., and K. Carley. 2005. "Structural Knowledge and Success of Anti-Terrorist Activity: The Downside of Structural Equivalence," *Journal of Social Structure* 6.

Uzzi, B., and S. Dunlap. 2005. "How to Build Your Network," *Harvard Business Review*, December.

Valente, T. 1996. "Social Network Thresholds in the Diffusion of Innovations," *Social Networks Journal* 18, Elsevier.

INDEX

3M, 20

Academy of Program/Project and
    Engineering Leadership
    (APPEL), 70–71
Accenture, 16–17, 62
administrative staff, developing social
    network with, 1–2
advice-seeking interactions: in case
    study, 41–42; circular diagram of,
    31, 32; mapped by NetMiner,
    36–37; mapped by UCINET/
    Netdraw, 34–36
affinity networks, 9
age diversity, 68
analogical reasoning, 11
The Art of Innovation (Kelley), 27
"Avoiding Being a Political Football"
    (Liebowitz), 27–28

Babson College, 52
baby boomer generation, 67

balanced scorecard, 92–93, 96, 107,
    109, 111
Best Manufacturing Practices, 71
betweenness, 34, 49, 54, 55
BI. *See* business intelligence (BI)
biotech firms, 73–74
blackboard.com, 4
blogs: for building personal
    knowledge networks, 7; for
    creating intelligence, 26–27;
    definition of, 26; example of, 26;
    for sharing knowledge, 7, 76
boomerang job, 72
Boston Consulting Group, 62
boundary spanners, 6–7, 9–10
bounded network approach, 33
Brain Technologies, 58
brainstorming, 11, 76
British Aerospace, 56–57
brokering roles, 9–10; and
    departmental communication,
    45–49; in producing strategic

intelligence, 29–30; social network
  analysis of, 32–33, 34, 39
building personas, 14
business intelligence (BI), 22–23, 24;
  definition of, 23; elements of, 23;
  knowledge management and, 23
Business Intelligence Summit, 23
business sector, social network
  analysis in, 73
Business Week, 13, 73

Carnegie Mellon University, 62, 69
carriers, 9, 32, 33, 47
central connectors, 9–10, 29
central position, 46, 47
change management, 19
chat rooms, 7
cheating, 16
chief executive officer (CEO),
  assistant to, 1–2
China, leadership qualities in, 13
circle network, 4, 5
cliques, 7
closeness, 34
coaching, 53
codification, 16–17
cohesion, 34, 43–44
cohesion index, 43
collaboration: in innovation, 13–15;
  and synergy, 28
collaborator, 14
College of Integrated Science and
  Technology, 15–16
communication: interdepartmental,
  44–45; intradepartmental, 43–44;
  measures of, 33–37; networks, 9;
  volume of, 42–43
competency management, 18–19
competitive intelligence (CI), 7,
  23–24; collecting, 23, 24;

definition of, 23
competitor capital, 19, 22
concept mapping, 59
conferences, 7
connectedness, 35
consolidated supervised entity
  (CSE), 103
context knowledge flow, 56, 57
"Creating a Culture for Innovation"
  (Ellis), 62
Cross, Rob, 9–10, 33, 52, 61–62, 63,
  69
cross-departmental meetings, 7
cross-functional teaming, 7
cross-generational knowledge flows,
  67–72; direction of, 70, 72;
  mapped by NetMiner, 55–56; in
  military and NASA, 70–72;
  programs for, 19, 71–72
cross-pollinator, 14
cross-staffing, 7
CSE. See consolidated supervised
  entity (CSE)

DaimlerChrysler, 14
declarative knowledge, 5–6
defense, social network analysis in, 73
Defense Intelligence Agency, 62
Delphi Group, 76
density, 34, 43–44
Department of Energy, 71
Development Dimensions
  International, 13
director, 14
discussion groups, 7
domination of networks, 63

education: knowledge sharing in,
  15–16; social network analysis in, 74
egocentric approach, 34

e-mails, 25
emeritus program, 71
employee advice-seeking
    interactions. *See* advice-seeking
    interactions
energy, in innovation, 61–62
Energy Policy Act (2005), 99
engineers, knowledge-sharing
    mentality of, 15
Enron, 69
entrepreneurship, 20
ethnographic analysis/observation, 38
Executive Resources Board (ERB),
    80, 81, 87, 90
expert process knowledge flow, 54, 55
expertise knowledge, 69
experts, 46–47
explicit knowledge, 5

facebook.com, 3, 9, 40, 74
facilitator of online community, 72
facilitators, 10
Fair Fund provision, 103
Federal Human Capital Survey, 106
fluid knowledge, 6
focus groups, 38
fragmentation of networks, 63
Friendster.com, 9

Gartner Group, 23
gatekeeper, 46
GEN3 Partners, Inc., 76
Google, 69
Government Accountability Office
    (GAO), 71, 79–116
grapevine (watercooler) effect, 12
group approach, 33

Hallmark, 14
Harvard Business Review, 40

Harvard University, 3
homeland security, social network
    analysis in, 73
human capital, 19, 22; strategy,
    18–19, 71, 79–116
Human Capital Assessment and
    Accountability Framework
    (HCAAF), 80, 85, 88, 90, 92, 96,
    106
Human Capital Review Board
    (HCRB), 80, 87, 89–95, 97, 103,
    111
hurdler, 14

IBM, 17–18, 40, 61; Business
    Consulting Services, 17–18;
    Institute for Business Value, 52;
    Research, 17–18
ideo.com, 13–14
in-degree centrality, 34
Indiana University, 16
InFlow, 62–63
information brokers, 9–10
information map, 52
innovation, 11–20; collaboration in,
    13–15; definition of, 11, 76;
    energy in, 61–62, 69; failure of,
    73; as goal-oriented process, 27;
    knowledge mapping and, 52–53;
    managing, 12–13; network biases
    against, 63; skills needed for, 73;
    steps in, 11–12, 61; "ten faces of,"
    13–14
"Innovation Survey Results" (Delphi
    Group), 76
innovative environment, 12–13, 62
Institute of Medicine, 74
institutional memory, 6
insularity, 63
integrated type of teaching, 15–16

intellectual capital, 19
intelligence. *See* business intelligence
    (BI); competitive intelligence
    (CI); strategic intelligence
interest-based networks, 9
International Network for Social
    Network Analysis (INSNA), 34, 40
International Sunbelt Social Network
    Conference, 40
internship programs, 17–18
interpersonal trust, 74
interviews, 38
intrapreneurship, 20
isolates, 9, 32, 33, 47
itinerant, 46

James Madison University, 15–16
job sharing, 72
Johns Hopkins University, 40, 41, 62
Journal of Social Structure, 40
jubilation, 12
junior–senior employee interactions,
    46, 68
junior–senior employee knowledge
    flows. *See* cross-generational
    knowledge flows

KM. *See* knowledge management
    (KM)
knowledge: application, 22; audits,
    31–32, 39, 51; capture, 22;
    capture/retention program, 72;
    categories of, 5–6; creation, 22,
    39, 62; fairs, 64; hoarding, 14–15,
    16; identification, 22; innovation,
    11; layers of, 69
knowledge management (KM):
    approaches in, 16–17; and
    business intelligence, 23; examples
    of, 16–17; failure of, 22; goals of,

22; and human capital strategy, 18;
    processes of, 22; and strategic
    intelligence, 22
Knowledge Management and
    Business Intelligence Workshop,
    23
knowledge maps, 51–59; definition
    of, 56; developing, 58–59;
    examples of, 53–57; forms of, 51;
    and innovation, 52–53; by
    Personal Brain, 57, 58; by SNA
    software, 34–37, 53–57
knowledge sharing, 22; blogs and
    wikis and, 26–27; constraints of,
    47–48; disciplines and cultural
    attitudes and, 15; factors of, 25;
    forums, 72; importance of, 12; and
    innovation, 14; vs. knowledge
    hoarding, 14–15, 16; paradigm
    shifts needed for, 15–18; research
    on, 25; trust and, 74; at World
    Bank, 64
Knowledge Xchange, 16–17

leadership qualities, 13
learning management system, 106
learning map, 52
learning personas, 13
length of service, 34, 36
Lessons-Learned Information
    System, 71
liaisons, 6, 29, 46
likability, 53
line network, 4, 5
LinkedIn.com, 9, 26, 40, 51, 76

mailing lists, 25
management: communication with,
    46; and human capital strategy,
    18–19; leadership qualities of, 13.

See also knowledge management (KM)
"Managing the Innovation Process" (Cummings), 12–13
Mars, Inc., 64–65
Massachusetts Institute of Technology, 12–13
medicine, social network analysis in, 74
mentoring programs, 7, 19, 36, 71
military, cross-generational knowledge flows in, 70–72
mind mapping, 59
multidimensional scaling, 34–35, 36
myspace.com, 40, 76

NASA: Academy of Program/Project Engineering Leadership of, 14; cross-generational knowledge flows in, 70–72; Engineering Network (NEN), 71; personal knowledge networks at, 8
National Academy of Public Administration, 82
National Innovation Act (2005), 62
National Security Agency, 68–69
Netdraw, 34–36, 40
NetMiner, 34, 36, 37, 40, 53–57
Network Roundtable, 52, 63

"The Office Chart That Really Counts" (McGregor), 61
Office of Administrative and Personnel Management, 80, 87, 90
Office of Administrative Services, 80, 85, 87, 90
Office of Compliance, Inspections, and Examinations (OCIE), 91, 100, 103

Office of Human Resources (OHR), 80, 82, 84, 87–113
Office of Management and Budget (OMB), 82, 85, 91, 96, 110, 113
Office of Personnel Management (OPM), 83, 85, 91, 94, 96, 101, 110, 113
Office of Public Utility Regulation (OPUR), 99
Office of Risk Assessment (ORA), 102
On Demand Innovation Services (ODIS), 17–18
online communities, 7, 14, 17, 25–27, 72
organizational trust, 74
organizing personas, 13–14
orgnet.com, 40
out-degree centrality, 34

PageRank system, 69
part-time retired annuitant/project team consultant, 71
performance management, 19
peripheral specialists, 9–10, 29, 32
personal approach, 34
Personal Brain, 57, 58
personal knowledge networks, 4–6; benefits of, 6; building, 6–8; definition of, 4; forms of, 4, 5; importance of, 8–9
personalization, 16–17
phased retirement, 19, 71
Post-It Notes, 20
postulation, 11
power position, 46, 47
proactive organization, 6
procedural knowledge, 5–6
process knowledge, 69
process knowledge flow, 54–56

professional societies, 7
"Profiles: The Real Value of Social
    Networks" (Li), 8–9
Protecting America's Competitive
    Edge Act, 62
Public Utility Holding Company Act
    (1935) (PUHCA), 99
"pull" approach, 6, 77
"push" approach, 6, 77

reactive organization, 6
receivers, 9, 32, 33, 47
rehearsal retirement, 72
Re-inventing the Corporation
    (Naisbitt and Auberdence), 20
relationship capital, 19, 22
relationship knowledge, 69
representative, 46
research, in innovation process, 11,
    12
respect, 2
response rate (survey), 38
retiree job bank, 71
ring network, 4, 5
risk, in innovative environment,
    12–13

sample size (survey), 38
Sarbanes-Oxley Act (2002), 81–82,
    84, 90, 103, 104
school, knowledge sharing in, 15–16
School of Informatics, 16
sciences, social network analysis in,
    73–74
scientists, knowledge-hoarding
    mentality of, 14–15
SCIP. See Society for Competitive
    Intelligence Professionals (SCIP)
Securities and Exchange Commission
    (SEC), 71, 79–116; creation of, 83;

GAO report on, 79–83; human
    capital management challenges at,
    84–85; staff and organization of,
    83–84; strategic human capital
    management at, 85–113
self-regulatory organizations (SRO),
    83
senior employees. See cross-
    generational knowledge flows
Sloan Management Review, 40
SLR. See student loan repayment
    (SLR)
Small Agency Council, 96
SMART, 58
snowball approach, 33
social network analysis (SNA),
    31–40; case study of, 41–48; for
    cross-generational knowledge
    flows, 19, 55–56, 67–72; definition
    of, 4, 31; development of, 31;
    education on, 40; examples of,
    17–18, 61, 63–65; identifying
    structural holes by, 12, 32, 39, 54;
    knowledge mapping and, 52–53;
    and knowledge sharing, 17–18;
    limitations of, 37–38; resources
    on, 40; software, NetMiner, 34,
    36, 37, 40, 53–57; software,
    UCINET/Netdraw, 34–36, 40;
    steps of, 33; uses of, 4, 31, 32,
    38–40, 62–63, 73–74
social network threshold model, 62
social networking: with
    administrative staff, 1–2; benefits
    of, 3–4; blog about, 26; forms of,
    1; and human capital strategy,
    18–19; and intrapreneurship, 20;
    and knowledge sharing, 16–18;
    through online communities, 7,
    14, 17, 25–27, 76; and strategic

intelligence, 21, 25–30, 77. *See also* innovation

social networks: biases of, 63; definition of, 3; mature, 8–9; for students, 3; types of, 2–3. *See also* brokering roles; personal knowledge networks

Social Networks (journal), 40

Society for Competitive Intelligence Professionals (SCIP), 7, 23–24

Society for Effective Lessons Learned Sharing, 71

sociograms, 74

Solvay, 61

SRO. *See* self-regulatory organizations (SRO)

star network, 4, 5

sticky knowledge, 6

storyteller, 14

storytelling, 64

strategic human capital management, 85–113

strategic intelligence, 21–30; definition of, 21; knowledge management and, 22, 24; social networking and, 21, 25–30, 77

strategic knowledge, 69

strategic knowledge flow, 54, 55–56

strategically important groups, 33–34

structural capital, 19, 22

structural holes, 12, 32, 39, 54

student loan repayment (SLR), 103, 105, 109, 110

surveys, 33, 38, 42

synergy, 4, 28

"syrupy" knowledge, 6

tacit knowledge, 5–6, 16–17, 22

teaching, integrated type of, 15–16

teleworking, 85, 103, 105, 108, 109, 110

"ten faces of innovation," 13–14

thematic groups, 63–64

transmitters, 9, 32, 33, 47

trust, 74

UCINET/Netdraw, 34–36, 40

United States, leadership qualities in, 13

University of Virginia, 9–10, 40, 52

value network analysis, 76

Washington Examiner, 67

watercooler (grapevine) effect, 12

"Who Knows Whom, and Who Knows What?" (Patton), 65

wikis, 26–27, 70, 76

work partners, 53

Working Knowledge Research Center, 52

workshops, 7

World Bank, 63–64

ABOUT THE AUTHOR

Jay Liebowitz is professor of information technology in the Carey Business School at Johns Hopkins University. He is also the program director of the graduate certificate program in competitive intelligence at Johns Hopkins University. He is the founder and editor in chief of *Expert Systems with Applications: An International Journal*, published by Elsevier. Previously, Dr. Liebowitz was the first knowledge management officer at NASA Goddard Space Flight Center, the Robert W. Deutsch Distinguished Professor of Information Systems at the University of Maryland, Baltimore County, chair of Artificial Intelligence at the U.S. Army War College, and professor of management science at George Washington University.

Dr. Liebowitz has published more than thirty books and over two hundred articles dealing with expert/intelligent systems, knowledge management, and information technology management. His newest books are *Strategic Intelligence: Business Intelligence, Competitive Intelligence, and Knowledge Management* (2006), *What They Didn't Tell You about Knowledge Management* (2006), *Communicating as IT Professionals* (2006), and *Addressing the Human Capital Crisis in the Federal Government: A Knowledge Management Perspective* (2004). He is the founder and chair of the World Congress on Expert Systems.

Dr. Liebowitz was a Fulbright Scholar, the IEEE-USA Federal Communications Commission Executive Fellow, and the International Association for Computer Information Systems' Computer Educator of the Year. He has consulted and lectured worldwide for numerous organizations. He can be reached at jliebow1@jhu.edu.